QUEER COWBOYS

QUEER COWBOYS

And Other Erotic Male Friendships in Nineteenth-Century American Literature

Chris Packard

QUEER COWBOYS
© Chris Packard, 2005, 2006.

All rights reserved. No part of this book may be used or reproduced in any manner whatsoever without written permission except in the case of brief quotations embodied in critical articles or reviews.

First published in hardcover in 2005 by
PALGRAVE MACMILLAN™
175 Fifth Avenue, New York, N.Y. 10010 and
Houndmills, Basingstoke, Hampshire, England RG21 6XS
Companies and representatives throughout the world.

PALGRAVE MACMILLAN is the global academic imprint of the Palgrave Macmillan division of St. Martin's Press, LLC and of Palgrave Macmillan Ltd. Macmillan® is a registered trademark in the United States, United Kingdom and other countries. Palgrave is a registered trademark in the European Union and other countries.

ISBN 978-1-4039-7597-3

Library of Congress Cataloging-in-Publication Data is available from the Library of Congress.

A catalogue record for this book is available from the British Library.

Design by Newgen Imaging Systems (P) Ltd., Chennai, India.

First PALGRAVE MACMILLAN paperback edition: March 2006

10 9 8 7 6 5 4 3 2 1

Transferred to Digital Printing in 2012

CONTENTS

List of Illustrations		vii
Acknowledgments		ix
Introduction		1
Chapter One	All-Male Queer Interracial Families in the Wilderness: James Fenimore Cooper Solves His Progeny Problem	19
Chapter Two	Rehearsing and Ridiculing Marriage in *The Virginian* and Other Adventure Tales	41
Chapter Three	American Satyriasis in Whitman, Harris, and Hartland	71
Chapter Four	"Queer Secrets" in Men's Clubs: Humor, Violence, and Homoerotic Elision in Works by Mark Twain, Bret Harte, and Eugene Field	95
Notes		119
Index		137

LIST OF ILLUSTRATIONS

1. "Cowboys around the Campfire" — 8
2. "A Hair-Cut à la Puncher," ink wash on paper — 10
3. "The JA Wagon Cook Taking a Shave," 1908 — 11
4. Three cowboys with cards and liquor, n.d. — 29
5. "Outdoor sleeping arrangements at the W.D. Boice Cattle Company" — 42
6. "Occ. Cowboys" posing on a tree trunk, 1904 — 46
7. "Cowboys Bathing in Pond" — 47
8. "Wister's Hunting Party in Camp at Jackson Hole, Wyoming, 1887" — 52
9. "Dance! You Short Horn Dance!" ink and transparent watercolor over graphite underdrawing on paper — 54
10. Frederic Remington's "Hello, Old Boy," illustrating a willowy young cowboy parting the flaps of the artist's tent — 58
11. "Dancing, seemingly not hampered by lack of women" — 72
12. "Pioneer Mining in California" — 73
13. "Two cowpunchers posed with their horses outside a saloon in Mexico" — 79
14. Walt Whitman styles himself as a "rough" on the frontispiece of *Leaves of Grass* (1855) — 90
15. "Cowboys Rolling Cigarettes, Comanche County" — 97
16. Cowboys dancing, flanked by band and woman with infant — 98

17. Mark Twain, shirtless, ca. 1883   106
18. Eugene Field and Francis Wilson   109
19. Facsimile of "Socratic Love," ink, graphite, and watercolor on vellum, 1888   113

ACKNOWLEDGMENTS

Thanks to the librarians, archivists, collectors, and interpreters of the American West who steered me toward manuscripts, objects, pictures, and indexes that revealed the evidence I use in this book. Most particularly, thanks to the Harry Ransom Humanities Research Center at the University of Texas at Austin for a 2001 fellowship and unlimited access to their collections; to those friends, family, and friends-of-family who let me stay in spare rooms during my research trips through Kansas, California, and Texas.

Writing is necessarily solitary, but my companions who generously gave suggestions are Lucienne Reed, Deborah Williams, Cyrus Patell, Mark Thompson, Sarah Johnson, Brita Servaes, Greg Anderson, Dameon Macnamara, Ron Caldwell, Matt Clark, Mark Tyler, Mike Muffoletto, Ann Brunjes, Hugh McGowan, Bruce Rinderman, Robert Doyle, Phillip Brian Harper, Dale Hrabi, Chris Schelling, John LaValle, Jack Booch, Cathy Lavender, and Kristi Long. For invaluable help with images, Don Sumada, Laura Foster, David Webb, Mike Anderson, Robert Flynt, and David Dietcher. A writer needs a room, and for generously providing housing assistance of various kinds, I humbly thank John Sugg, Matt Goldman, George Talmadge Grigsby, Basil Racuk, Jim Hoffman, Scott Hamm, Gene Mignola, Richard Sacks, the Kennedys, the Wrights, the Cahills, the Comptons, and the Keiths. Essential encouragement came from Clyde Martin, Sam Pendleton, Kevin Wells, Don Pitkin, Russ Virani, Priscilla Rodgers, and the entire swim team.

INTRODUCTION

Think *cowboy*, and what image comes to mind? The Marlboro man? The Lone Ranger? Matt Dillon? These men are icons, and their images are recognized around the world as symbols of American masculinity. Ruggedly handsome men of few words and calculated actions, they epitomize the strong, silent type that has for more than 150 years been associated with the freedoms of wide-open spaces in the American West. If you look a little closer at this image, you'll see another figure, the cowboy's sidekick—his partner and loyal friend. Together they ride the range, making or breaking laws. This book is about the bonds that hold this pair together, particularly the erotic affection that undergirds their friendship.

Today, images of cowboys come from movies and television, but before 1900, the originals from which these famous icons derive their type appeared in print, years before broadcast media had been invented. The cattle herder on the open prairies first appeared in the popular press in 1863, and soon dominated the literary marketplace. Sensationalistic cowboy tales sold far more copies than similar frontier tales about fur trappers, lumberjacks, miners, cavalrymen, Indian fighters, and scouts. Beadle and Adams and other mass-market publishers in New York and Philadelphia between the 1860s and the 1890s churned out tale after tale of the "blood and thunder" Westerns featuring cowboys named Seth Jones, Nick Carter, Buffalo Bill, and Bijah Buck. Using newly invented printing technologies and inexpensive "pulp" paper, these flimsy, luridly printed cardboard-and-newsprint volumes cost just pennies apiece and were widely available by subscription, at corner newsstands, and at railroad and streetcar depots. In the years following the Civil War, when the entire nation looked westward for the fulfillment of American promises, the popular press promoted a wide-open region, wholly imagined, populated not by men but by legends, where thrilling adventures tested the metal of Anglo-American resolve.

Explosive sales and numerous reprintings in several languages ensured a vast readership. Each Western was drenched with the sensationalistic prose, flat melodramatic characters, and repetitive cliffhanger structures that have come to characterize the Western as a literary genre.[1]

Owen Wister's *The Virginian* was published in 1901. This classic cowboy tale is often credited with lifting a second-rate literary genre to the heights of the classics. Although it was just the sort of romance that Henry James would have hated, he praised it lavishly: "Bravo, bravo," he wrote in a note to Wister, "you have made him [the Virginian] *live* with a high but lucid complexity."[2] Not only did it garner praise from an influential critic, but Wister's book was also popular in terms of sales, a blockbuster to an almost unprecedented degree. It went through 15 reprintings in eight months. Although Wister published many other books, some about the American West, and some not, he was always remembered as the author of "that book," the one about the cowboy, the bad guy, and the schoolmarm. This is the formula that most Westerns of the twentieth century adhered to, whether in print, radio, or film.

A folk hero, the cowboy embodies the most precious values in the nation: unrestricted freedom, crafty self-reliance, familiarity with wilderness and horses, good with guns. A savior often of what he deems good, a tireless vanquisher of what he decides is bad, the cowboy's quest teaches boys and men to emulate a cluster of behaviors, values, actions, and frames of reference that connote idealized manhood. Ruggedness, ingenuity, and fearlessness are all qualities the cowboy embodies, while feminine qualities such as domesticity, weakness, and purity are anathema to his unwritten masculine code.

Some aspects of cowboy masculinity are more suggestive of a rapscallion than a Dudley Do-Right. No matter who does the measuring, the cowboy in pre-1900 literature is not an upstanding example of social responsibility. He is usually profoundly misogynistic; he makes a mockery of established religion. He is a spendthrift and a cheat. He is a racist agent of U.S. imperialism. And he practices the hygiene and habits of a tomcat. Still, for large numbers of American consumers of culture, then and now, the cowboy is to be forgiven his antisocial and aggressively rebellious behaviors. His renegade attitude is exactly the quality that Americans most appreciate in this hero. Audiences want the cowboy "out there" on the frontier,[3] stirring up trouble. Without a wife or children, without domestic possessions, without social status of any kind, the cowboy is "free" in the sense that he adheres to no law but his own. He is a bowdlerized figure of Ralph Waldo Emerson's ideal American, governed not by books or received ideas but by whim and an unmediated relationship with nature.

Some have called this figure an American Adam, living in peaceful cohabitation in the wilderness, a neo-Rousseauian savage; still others, a dastardly rapist of virgin landscapes who massacres Indians, Mexicans, and buffalo in the name of Manifest Destiny. In all these interpretations, scant attention has been given to the rather wide variety of sexual and erotic discourses used and practiced by cowboys and other frontiersmen while they are "out there" on the frontier. Most people, if they think about it at all, assume that the cowboy in history and in literature practiced sexual abstention until he arrived in a town, where he practiced the acceptable vice of dalliances with female prostitutes. But this explanation is counterintuitive and is not supported in the literary record. Particularly in Westerns produced before 1900, references to lusty passions appear regularly, when the cowboy is on the trail with his partners, if one knows how to look for them. In fact, in the often all-male world of the literary West, homoerotic affection holds a favored position. A cowboy's partner, after all, is his one emotional attachment, aside from his horse, and he will die to preserve the attachment. Affection for women destroys cowboy *comunitas* and produces children, and both are unwanted hindrances to those who wish to ride the range freely.

In other words, the cowboy is queer: he is odd; he doesn't fit in; he resists community; he eschews lasting ties with women but embraces rock-solid bonds with same-sex partners; he practices same-sex desire. His code permits few "norms" as defined by his audience of working-class Anglo-American men, but his popularity grants him wide latitude in terms of exercising his queer power. Before 1900, that is to say before the modern invention of the "homosexual" as a social pariah, cowboy narratives represented male–male affection quite a bit more freely than Westerns produced after 1900, when male–male sex was classified as abnormal. *Queer Cowboys* investigates these originary texts, beginning with those of James Fenimore Cooper in the 1820s and ending with Wister's *The Virginian* of 1901. I hope to teach readers how to recognize homoerotic affection in a historical discourse that was free from the derogatory meanings associated with post-1900 evaluations of male–male erotic friendships.

Fifty years ago, in an essay entitled "Come Back to the Raft Ag'in, Huck Honey!," Leslie Feidler argued that such well-known nineteenth-century American classics as *Huckleberry Finn*, *Moby Dick*, *The Leatherstocking Tales*, and *Two Years Before the Mast* depict fantasies of outcast white juvenile males, orphans in the wilderness, seeking and finding erotic but unconsummated love in the arms of adult male slaves, Indians, and cannibals. Predictably, Feidler's essay caused a sensation. According to Ralph Ellison, calling the friendship between Huckleberry Finn and Jim "homosexual" was the same as "yell[ing] out his most terrifying name for chaos."[4] In language that today seems dishonest and sensationalistic, Feidler blames "the existence of homosexuality" as a threat to privileged males-only spaces, where nonsexual, friendly "camaraderie" between men enjoys unsuspicious intimacy:

> The existence of overt homosexuality threatens to compromise an essential aspect of American sentimental life: the camaraderie of the locker-room and ball park, the good fellowship of the poker game and fishing trip, a kind of passionless passion, at once gross and delicate, homoerotic in the boy's sense, possessing an innocence above suspicion.[5]

Feidler's essay appeared three years after the end of World War II, and his derogatory use of words such as "fag" and "queer" elsewhere in his essay recall a thoughtless, pre–Civil Rights Era speech pattern that assumes "overt homosexuality" is a hostile challenge to intimate but nonsexual male friendships. Feidler believed that nonsexual bonhomie deserves protection. Of course Feidler's fears are ridiculous. Huck and Jim's friendship on the raft might be erotic, but how could it be "homosexual" when the word hadn't been invented yet?[6]

What makes the friendship between a runaway boy and a slave in the 1840s perennially interesting, as James Looby has pointed out, is that it can't be mapped onto contemporary understandings about same-sex intimate friendships. Uncontained by the prison of twenty-first-century meanings, Huck's and Jim's relationship on the raft, idealized in sensuous language and depicted as sometimes highly erotic, refuses the categories that readers today know so well. Instead, Twain attempted to capture a friendship that could have occurred along the Mississippi River before the Civil War, and if his book is realistic, then the erotic bonds described in it must be accurate in a historical sense. Sexual liasons between female slaves and white men in this region during this period are amply documented in fiction as well as in fact. However, historical records of male–male sexual encounters along the Mississippi River during this period include erotic letters written by Southerners and Civil War soldiers, some suggestive dialogue in Minstrel shows, and a handful of newspaper accounts of arrests for "sodomy."[7] Given this historical evidence, it is not hard to believe that Jim's affectionate petting, their nudity, and Huck's appreciative remembrances of their ideal life on the raft are realistic.

Today in America, when every teenager learns how not to be gay, it is difficult to suspend prejudice while looking at erotic male friendships in - history. Without much evidence to go on, the contours of same-sex erotic intimacies in the nineteenth century are difficult to recognize. However, when the evidence comes from literature, the contours are visible and the emotional qualities of same-sex desire can be discerned. In almost all frontier tales, and at the center of the most popular and best loved of these tales, homoerotic friendships preserve privilege and ensure survival in a hostile wilderness. How these bonds work to further the interests of Anglo-American males in the late nineteenth century is the subject of *Queer Cowboys*.

Westerns are well known for their stereotypes of ethnic warfare, valorizing whites and demonizing nonwhites. Again and again the dominant narrative renders the threat of "savagery" upon the whites as a just motive for racist domination and acquisition of territory and resources. It is a narrative strategy as old as Enlightenment-era Colonialism. *Queer Cowboys* looks beneath this dominant narrative in Westerns to find simultaneous narratives of intimacy between Anglos and non-Anglos, updating Leslie Feidler's stale claims for "innocent" homosexuals suffering from arrested development. Following the model of James Fenimore Cooper, Westerns and sea tales often include secret friendships, even marriage rituals, between representatives of warring groups, intimate bonds that are based on shared values and resources. Dime and half-dime novels, in particular, feature young white boys, usually orphans, befriended by certain natives and tutored in the ways of the wilderness. Rituals of brotherhood, including exchanges of blood, and elaborate physical nuptial-like rituals are common in these friendships, which offer an alternative to the dominant theme of ethnic warfare.

Such tales amount to parables teaching the Anglo that his enemy is his friend, and the ways of "the savage" make sense in wilderness contexts. Familial relations between ethnically different men, interracial brotherhood, are synecdoches for citizenship in an idealized territory where femininity is excluded, and differences in race or citizenship are eliminated, illustrating a potential solution to the ethnic and sexist warfare of the dominant narrative. That these bonds are sometimes betrayed in these tales of conquest, betrayed in the name of U.S. national race hegemony, is a trigger for race warfare of the most pernicious kind, saturated as it is with regret for spoiling what was once unified but must be split in the name of "civilization."

In the startling words of Walter Benn Michaels, male–male sexual and affectionate pairing in American literary culture offers "a solution to the problem of heterosexuality."[8] The problem he speaks of is the threat of reproductivity through miscegenation in a period when fear of ethnic mixing through marriage or sex was especially keen in American culture. This fear contends with nationalistic rhetoric conceiving citizenship in terms of a single idealized family. The solution, Michaels argues, appears in several literary idealizations of incestuous interracial bachelor families that explore erotic relationships but never produce children through conventional channels. These relations are fantasies that permit total intimacy along with total ethnic purity, "independent of and so unthreatened by the deracinating potential of femininity" (48). Michaels limits his discussion to modern American literature of the 1920s and 1930s, a generation after the heyday of the Western, but he establishes a theoretical link between ethnic difference and the homoerotic discourse that *Queer Cowboys* extends to pre-1900 literature.

A new look at some familiar texts reveals that what Owen Wister calls "the elemental talk of sex" is a central theme in most well-known cowboy tales and other conquest narratives of the nineteenth century. Far from being silent on the subject of sexuality, those who wrote about nineteenth-century frontiersmen associated these icons of American masculinity with exuberant erotic expression. If manhood in the genre of Western can be defined by reactions to violence from enemies, as Richard Slotkin and Ogdgen Nash Smith have argued, then it can also be measured by the strength of affection for the ubiquitous loyal sidekick who accompanies the hero on his quest, which critics have failed to point out.[9] Yet almost every Western includes a love story between friends drawn together under dire circumstances. This friendship inspires the roistering cowboy to live up to communal standards without relinquishing his identity as a nomad. Same-sex bonds permit the universal human need for companionship and stability in an often hostile or chaotic wilderness, but because there are neither domestic nor reproductive consequences, the intimate friendship does not hinder the cowboy's spontaneity.

In action-packed Westerns, discussions about sex, and sex acts themselves, appear far less frequently than sudden avalanches, surprising encounters with grizzlies, nighttime stampedes, sneaky Indians or thieving Mexicans, which drench nearly every page of Westerns. Even so, Andy Adams devotes a few pages of *The Log of a Cowboy: A Narrative of the Old Trail Days* (1903) to what the cowboys call "the mastering passion."[10] Around the campfire, after a hard day of riding, the elder cowboys talk about their failed amorous affairs with women expressly to educate those younger boys "who have not experienced the tender passion" (72). The stories they don't tell, but that readers and younger cowboys perceive, is about the closeness of a group of men around a campfire. A litany of broken hearts, bad timing, or insurmountable obstacles cause each storyteller to give up the whole business of courtship, to reject normative rituals governing desire, and to reject civilization itself. One cowboy tries to marry a rich girl in Kentucky, but his humble origins are unacceptable (78). Another rejects a girl he likes because her brother is rude: "I ought to have shot him and checked the breed," he gripes. Instead he simply refuses his beloved, essentially accomplishing the same thing.[11] Time and again cowboys report that they have tried but failed with women. They just can't seem to create convincing language about the worthiness of women for their passions.

When it comes to male camaraderie, on the other hand, each cowboy always knows just what to do. "Honest" John Glen reports that "the reason he did n't marry [a widow] was, he was too honest to take advantage of a dead man" (82), so he stuck to the bachelor life. With a wink, this cowboy reveals his fidelity to a dead man as the source of his refusal to marry. The message for younger members of the outfit in *The Log of a Cowboy* is that the normalizing function of marriage to women, and the domesticating

Illustration 1 According to Andy Adams, 1903 in *The Log of a Cowboy*. Late-night campfire tales between cowboys were usually about failed relationships with women and testimonials of loyalty to all-male cowboy culture, "Cowboys around the campfire" by Erwin E. Smith. Library of Congress accession number LC-S6-89.

influence of femininity, is a deal-breaker for those following the cowboy code. Their status as cowboys relies upon bachelorhood, not a solitary hermit's isolation but something formed around a partnership. This friendship is based upon an unspoken attachment resembling, a blood tie, and involving loyalty, but not fidelity. Their tales of failures with women justify their emotional attachments to a cowboy outfit, an outfit in which each partner shares a bedroll and a string of horses with another.

Jane Tompkins in *West of Everything* concludes that Westerns of the late nineteenth century, with their unapologetic exclusion of femininity and their laconic hero-with-a-checkered-past, are reactionary narratives, competing with the then-popular sentimental-domestic novels that were flooding the marketplace and promoting ideals of female influence in the sphere of the home. Instead of domestic plots and the conventions of "women's novels," Westerns of the nineteenth century feature violence and turgid action as the lingua franca, reserving discussions of love and loyalty to the margins and minimal language.[12]

Badger C. Clark's poem "The Lost Pardner" mourns the loss of "Al," his long-term partner, in language suggestive of both spiritual and physical homoeroticism:

> And him so strong, and yet so quick he died,
>   And after year on year
> When we had always trailed it side by side,
>   He went—and left me here!
> We loved each other in the way men do
>   And never spoke about it, Al and me,
> But we both *knowed*, and knowin' it so true
>   Was more than any woman's kiss could be.
> We knowed—and if the way was smooth or rough,
>   The weather shine or pour,
> While I had him the rest seemed good enough—
>   But he ain't here no more![13]

The erotic implications of this unspoken love lie in the remembrance, "I wait to hear him ridin' up behind / And feel his knee rub mine in the good old way." Clark's approximate rhyme of "ridin' " and "behind" and "mine" suggests that what Al's knee rubs is perhaps not just the speaker's knee. His mournful lyric recalls a love that enjoyed a privileged status pointed out by an intransitive verb form of knowing—"we both *knowed*" (emphasis in original), as if what both knew could go without saying.

Queer theory as developed by Eve Kosofsky Sedgwick, Jonathan Dollimore, and Lee Edelman posits that erotic desire between men essentially erases identity, since it subverts the traditional subject/object praxis that undergirds presumptions about heterosexual desire. The poet and Al *know* without speaking. In other words, when a cowboy desires his partner, he desires himself, destabilizing an essential given in male/female constructions of desire rooted in oppositions. Cowboy literature and other adventure tales of the nineteenth century are excellent places to locate the residues of these unspoken but known homoerotic desires. Liberated from the hearth-bound restrictions implied by male–female pairs, cowboys are

Illustration 2 Frederic Remington's illustrations include intimacies between cowboy partners that need not be explained in language, but speak of homoerotic unions in gesture, line, and shadow. "A Hair-Cut à la Puncher," ink wash on paper. By Frederic Remington. North Carolina Museum of Art, Raleigh, Gift of the Frank R. Penn family in memory of Roberta Winton Penn.

free to indulge their desires with partners who require no dialectical or oppositional constitutive identity. Cowboys are famous for resisting just such strictures; in desiring his partner, the cowboy erases distinctions, removing the need to explain or define the urgencies of intimacy or the sources of passion in a friendship. "We loved each other the way men do," writes Badger Clark, "and never spoke about it." But even without speech,

Illustration 3 Cowboy intimacy takes shape here in a carefully arranged photograph telling a story that could include eroticism. "The JA Wagon Cook Taking a Shave, JA Ranch, Texas. Rovert Faure ('Frenchy') Does the Shaving," 1908. Nitrate negative, by Erwin E. Smith. Amon Carter Museum, Ft. Worth, Texas, accession number LC-S59-17.

both cowboys in Clark's poem know through physical contact that their love is "more than any woman's kiss could be." The desire expressed in the language is embedded in gestures, imagery, and figurative codes. *Queer Cowboys* decodes these unspoken and, until now, unrealized messages.

Queer Cowboys contributes to an ongoing intellectual movement called The New Western History, which seeks to balance the traditional views of the American West—essentially a monolithic conquest model best articulated in Frederick Jackson Turner's essay on the closing of the American frontier—with more diverse, more localized, more ethnically representative perspectives. Historians such as Patricia Nelson Limerick and literary scholars such as Jane Tompkins, Blake Allmendinger, and William Handley have promoted The New Western History, and my project contributes to their efforts by inviting enthusiasts of Westerns and gay studies to imagine the sexual and erotic lives of cowboys and others of the "Old West" period. *Queer Cowboys* works to reframe discussions about popular culture in nonnormative terms and presents archival records—some familiar, some never seen before—as evidence of nonnormative practices. These records refute orthodox views of Western history. Instead, they reveal support patterns in literary texts suggesting diverse, if not deviant, ways of expressing affection in wilderness contexts.

The cowboys around the campfire in Andy Adams's *The Log of a Cowboy* tacitly agree to reject normative desires that lead to families, preferring instead the company of their own kind, and this agreement is erotic. Al, in Clark's "The Lost Pardner," knows a silent language that is buried in implied intimacies and unnamed knowledge beyond a woman's kiss. These unspoken but erotic bonds deserve attention because they suggest the cowboy *comunitas* is in part organized around same-sex practices or desires. Although a loner, the cowboy is never really alone. His partner always consoles him. Given the instant and undying popularity of cowboys in U.S. popular culture during a period of rapid national expansion, to identify a homoerotic core in its myth about the supremacy of white American masculinity is to imply that American audiences want their frontiersmen to practice nonnormative desires as part of their roles in nation building. In other words, if there is something national about the cowboy (and other frontier heroes of his ilk), and if there is something homoerotic about the partnerships he forms in the wilderness, then there is something homoerotic about American national identity as it is conceived in the literary West.

The typical cowboy narrative—told and re-told, imaged and re-imaged almost continually since 1870—speaks powerfully to the nation's fantasy about its men; the hero of this national fantasy embodies its most cherished values and ideals. Often the frontiersman's single redeeming virtue is his willingness to express loyalty and affection to a partner. A cure to violence, to endlessly beset manhood, is same-sex affection. His lone virtue and also sometimes his Achilles' heel is his loyalty to his partner. Again and again in narratives of conquest, whether on the high seas or the high desert, whether on the wrong side of the law or on the right, survival in often hostile territory depends upon devotion to his partner. These same-sex partnerships are typical of cowboy narratives, and *Queer Cowboys* inspects the qualities that hold them together.

What do cowboys talk about when they talk about sex? How do they explain the gaps between their desires and the expectations of the East coast establishment? If there is an erotic connection created when these paragons of masculinity confess inexperience with "the great mastering passion," what does it look or sound like, and what social or aesthetic function does it serve? The chapters that follow document instances in pre-1900 American literature of homoerotic discourses and analyze these representations. Some texts such as James Fenimore Cooper's *The Leatherstocking Tales*, Owen Wister's *The Virginian*, or Walt Whitman's poetry are well known and have always been the subject of analysis. Others such as Claude Hartland's confession of a sexual odyssey in *The Story of a Life*, Frank Harris's *My Reminiscences as a Cowboy*, Frederic Loring's *Two College Friends*, or Eugene Field's "Socratic Love," are less well known and have never been mined for their language about homoeroticism. Within canonical as well as ignored literature, high culture as well as low, homoerotic intimacy is not only present, but it is also thematic in works produced before the modern invention of the vice labeled "homosexuality." The cowboy is queer because audiences want him to be queer. America's official emblem of masculinity is not one who settles down after he conquests, as does the mythos of the equivalent figure in European culture; rather, he moves on, perpetually conquering, and repeatedly affirming his ties to the wilderness and his male partner.

The erotic lives of men in Westerns can be divided into two categories: the physical and the emotional/spiritual. Neither engages in erotic relations with femininity, whether expressed by a man or a woman. Of the physical aspects of eroticism, Bruce Seiberts in his memoir *Nothing but Prairie and Sky* recalls that cowboys on the trail "had a general idea that our sex hunger was caused by such a heavy meat diet, but I never heard of anyone going vegetarian because of this."[14] Seiberts describes "sex hunger" in the first person plural, "our," as if all cowboys share a common sex hunger, which is easily explained as a consequence of eating meat. The correlation between eating meat and "sex hunger" rests upon an anthropomorphic view associating men with beasts, linking consumption of meat with a subsequent physical arousal. Seiberts's wry observation about vegetarians implies that no self-respecting cowboy would avoid meat in order to avoid an erection, even without females around to rut with. In fact, since sex-for-procreation is suicide for a cowboy's bachelor identity, one who claims his sex hunger practically invites what contemporary sociologists call "situational homosexuality," such as the kind practiced in prisons, military barracks, and locker rooms.

When Seiberts uses "sex hunger" to describe an erection, he suggests an archaic and perhaps sanitized vocabulary. Western tales and memoirs published for the mass market before 1900 are invariably euphemistic when deploying language about sex. But in privately printed verse, when the readership is exclusively male, one Denver journalist in the 1880s calls his erection a "codger" or a "three-cornered yelper," which he uses to "Rasp, roger, diddle, bugger, screw, canoodle, kife, and mow."[15] The suggestion of a tumid phallus in Westerns produced before 1900, however carefully coded, is nearly always present. In fact, the prose style of Westerns is inflated, pompous, and fulsome. Their frothy plots and racy language enacts the tumescence that the pumped-up friendship promises. My point here is that a cowboy's "sex hunger" and its family of meanings describes the drive of the cowboy pushed by his audiences to conquer, to explore, and to create the tumult in the wilderness that predicts change, that lies beyond the boundaries and carves new spaces in the presumed chaos of wilderness, spaces that East coast American culture can later inhabit and populate through normative male–female breeding that produces children.

The frontiersman is moved by his "sex hunger," his tumescence, to seek beyond the culture's boundaries. In this sense, he is a penetrator of wilderness, but he is not, as many critics argue, a pre-sexual figure typologically related to Adam before the Fall, nor a sexually abstinent adolescent who is emotionally (but not sexually) attached to nonwhite "savages."[16] Instead, the cowboy's popularity can be explained by his appeal as a horny pantheist, whose antecedents are the Greek hero-lovers; but unlike the harmonious twin-lovers of ancient myth such as Achilles and Patroclus, American cowboys seek partners whose essence lies in difference of race, difference of national or tribal allegiance, but not difference of gender.

A second aspect of male–male eroticism in Westerns of this period is not the temporary release of sexual energy after a satisfying meal, but the intense and often lifelong partnerships of the kind that Feidler mistakenly calls nonsexual. Male marriage in nineteenth-century American literature is usefully compared to the "Boston Marriage" as described by Lillian Faderman in *Surpassing the Love of Men*. Named after the first feminists of Boston's "bluestocking" neighborhood, the Boston Marriage connotes same-sex cohabitation by vigorous and urbane intellectual women, who rejected the option to marry men and instead shared economic, social, and domestic resources, as well as the same bed, with like-minded women.[17] Unlike Boston Marriages, cowboy partnerships occur exclusively outside of communities, but their bonds include shared emotional intimacy, mutual affection, spiritual correspondences, and physical closeness. Most of James Fenimore Cooper's tales of the wilderness, whether in the woods, the plains, or upon the high seas, feature male partnerships that resemble marriages, but which deviate in important ways from this model. For example, the partners are usually racially different, or they are enemies from warring factions. Their erotic bonds make sense in the wilderness, where they create families by acquiring foundling biracial children, but in conventional social settings among Anglo-American elites, these all-male incestuous and interracial family structures cannot exist. Cooper's novels make space for these alternative family structures, experimenting with possible ways of hybridizing Anglos with Indians, or Anglos with Africans, or British with Americans without polluting racial purity.

Cooper's fiction is in every sense original, spawning the entire industry of dime novel adventure tales. Nearly half a century after Cooper's tales appeared, Owen Wister re-invented and re-invigorated the cowboy tale with *The Virginian*, where men of different classes—one a savvy but illiterate cowboy, the other an erudite, clueless Greenhorn—rehearse the marriage rituals before the cowboy hitches his wagon to the schoolmarm at the end of the book. Male marriage is also a feature of several now-forgotten novels of the 1870s and 1880s, including *Two College Friends, Live Boys; or Charlie and Nasho in Texas, The Texas Matchmaker* and *Bijah Buck and his Queer Find*.

I have divided the chapters that follow into separate investigations of two aspects of male–male erotic friendships: male marriage leading to interracial all-male families, and tumescence and its implications. The spontaneous, temporary sexual union—the expression of "sex hunger" without reproductive consequences—finds no stronger voice than in Walt Whitman's poetry. His commentary on the West stands out in this period as the single greatest literary work celebrating tumescence and linking it to a radically new literary aesthetic. Echoes of this homoerotic aesthetic, which I call American satyriasis, appear in Frank Harris's autobiography of sexual and literary awakenings in Kansas in the 1870s, and Claude Hartland's little-known confessions of a sex addict in St. Louis in the 1890s. Finally, a look at Mark Twain's and Eugene Field's sub-rosa literary output, explicitly written for an all-male audience by these two Western wits, celebrates with surprising frankness the appeal of the erect phallus.

Did Seiberts satisfy his "sex hunger" after a meal? Did he satisfy it with other hungry cowboys? Did Huck and Jim have sex in their wigwam on the raft? Did the narrator of *The Log of a Cowboy* indulge in physical intimacy with his bedroll partner after their campfire confessions? For the sake of argument, let's go ahead and assume that they did. What evidence of these acts remains for the historian? No children are produced, few civic documents except the sheriff's or marshal's records recognize the kinds of desires that compel such sex acts. Only a handful of homoerotic love letters have yet come to light, and newspaper accounts of "sodomy" are rare. A recent search of the Dodge City Police Court Docket, 1885–1888, reveals evidence of male prostitutes arrested during a sweep of what were termed "houses of ill-fame and assignation." On the same night, both "Howard Hines" and "John Smith" paid a $5.00 fine plus $7.50 court costs for being "an inmate of a house of ill fame": language that is identical to that used for "Myrtle Glover" and "Mabel Watson." Other men arrested on the same date were charged with "vagrancy" and fined $10.00. Why did the court single out Hines and Smith from other men arrested that night and convict them of identical crimes as two female prostitutes? Why did Hines and Smith pay the fines and admit their guilt?

The dearth of historical evidence should not be construed as the absence of it. After all, until Philip Durham and Everett Jones presented their evidence in *The Negro Cowboys* in 1965, most assumed that cowboys were predominantly white, when in fact as many as 40 percent of all cattle workers were African Americans in the "Old West" period immediately following the Civil War.[18] Still ignored today is the debt that cowboy culture owes to *vaqueros* and *californios*, those skilled Mestizo horsemen of 1830s who inhabited the regions now known as Northern Mexico and the southwestern United States, and whose lexicon and cultural practices were adopted wholesale by the Anglo immigrants.

Historians have yet to document the sex lives of the first cowboys.[19] Clifford P. Westermeier's 1976 article, "The Cowboy and Sex," is the single exception, and his anecdotal report avoids analysis and assumes that cowboys either had sex with women or not at all. Journalistic accounts of whorehouse shenanigans reveal, Westermeier argues, a "foul-mouthed, drunk, corrupt, and lecherous" (86) figure while carousing in the boomtowns along the cattle trail, but a sexually abstinent "hard-working, dedicated, and fun-loving man on the range, or in the camps, where women, cards, and rum were conspicuously absent" (87). Blake Allmendinger denies a history of sex acts between cowboys in history but outlines an iconic discourse of managing sex acts between animals that is anything but normative, with its violent neutering practices and branding rituals.

Recently, other kinds of historical evidence have emerged, other anecdotes suggesting that homoerotic cultures thrived in certain pre-1900 Anglo, Mestizo, and Native American communities in the West, cultures that were organized around male–male sexual practices and behaviors. For example, Williams and Roscoe find references to *berdache* figures in almost all the Great Plains Native American tribes. *Berdache* is the French term for two-spirited shaman of various indigenous tribes, male Indians who undergo a ritual transformation after which they live as women, marry, and provide spiritual leadership for the tribe. Anthropological evidence suggests that certain male–male sex acts in Mexican cultures, while common, do not implicate the inserter in an identity associated with the act. C. Michael Quinn's recent study of homoerotic cultures in nineteenth-century Mormon communities reveals much about the way same-sex sexual encounters were both policed and encouraged through church and civic institutions in the territory of Utah. Literary historians such as Gifford and Ullman have uncovered documents testifying to Victorian era intersex communities and other deviant sexualities in Europe and the United States. And Jonathan Ned Katz's *Gay American History* has uncovered thousands of overlooked documents testifying to homosexual histories in the United States, while just half-dozen depict such histories in the frontier West.

The following chapters demonstrate many instances of male erotic friendships in Westerns. These partnerships provide loving counterpoints to the violence of the wilderness. From dime novels to literary gems like *The Virginian*, writers depict frontier partnerships as primary, dynamic, and loving. Emotional bonds, social bonds, and physical bonds characterize these same-sex friendships, not to mention a great deal of unguarded affection and, I argue, erotic attraction. With the threat of violence on every side, male affection becomes not only erotic but also heroic, charged with the special swelling meaning of eros. The bonds between men promote tumescence, and even lifelong marriage, without the threat of losing the special status of cowboy by being burdened with a family.

CHAPTER ONE

ALL-MALE QUEER INTERRACIAL FAMILIES IN THE WILDERNESS

James Fenimore Cooper
Solves His Progeny Problem

James Fenimore Cooper pioneered the use of distinctive American scenes and idioms as central motifs in fiction. Before 1800, popular literature in the United States emulated European fare, often set in far-away places and times. Along with Charles Brockden Brown, Catherine Maria Sedgwick, and Washington Irving, Cooper began describing local scenery, figures in recent memory such as George Washington and John Paul Jones, and the provincial concerns of Anglo-American citizens. His influence on American literary and popular culture is difficult to overstate. With *The Pioneers* in 1823, he invented the frontiersman as a folk hero, the literary forefather of such popular legends of the nineteenth century as Kit Carson, Deadwood Dick, and Nick of the Woods. Even such twentieth-century icons as The Lone Ranger and Tonto, or the white/Indian partnerships in any number of filmed Westerns from Hollywood, owe their familiarity to Cooper's originals. With *The Pilot* in 1824, Cooper invented the sea tale, staking out the literary territory that Melville, Stoddard, and Conrad would later find so productive. Almost any action-adventure story in the 200-year history of the United States—stories of American masculinity triumphing over, well, almost everything—can be traced to Cooper's two-dozen tales of the sea and the North American wilderness.[1] Many of them were best sellers, earning Cooper a fortune and an unprecedented degree of celebrity status in the United States and Europe. Cooper's stories about wise but illiterate frontiersmen of the prairie, or the dashing defenders of democracy on the high seas, have been republished, re-told, and re-formatted to various media in the 150 years since then, most recently in a 1992 blockbuster version of *The Last of the Mohicans* starring Daniel Day Lewis.[2]

Critics then and now agree that Cooper's characters are idealizations, not realistic, in spite of his claims in almost every preface to represent reality accurately. His Indians had "no living prototype in our forests," according to General Lewis Cass, an Indian fighter, in 1828. Readers today who remember Cooper's fiction recall its stilted style, not his vivid characters. Most would agree with Mark Twain, who accuses Cooper of creating "personages" that fail to resemble real people in any way. Cooper did not even attempt realism, according to D.H. Lawrence, because he was writing myth, an original American myth. He created the first frontiersman in order to say something about white masculinity in America before 1850. Cooper placed this mythical figure in the North American wilderness in a not-so-far-away time before the American Revolution. And Cooper invented for his frontiersman a brawny, usually silent Indian, a chief of the Delaware tribe. This friendship between white and Indian, dramatized against a backdrop of a fantasy wilderness, tells an important story about how Anglo-Americans ought to value their most powerful men. Their story in the woods, their bonds, their "intercourse" to use Cooper's term, had never before appeared in literature.[3] The instant and lasting popularity of these tales are testaments to their importance in American popular culture.

Myths teach individuals in a culture what is valued and how to achieve it, and for Americans reading James Fennimore Cooper's books, the lessons about these "two childless, womanless men, of opposite races," who in D.H. Lawrence's opinion have a relationship "deeper than the deeps of sex," represent "the inception of a new humanity." Lawrence skims over the question of sex by placing the frontiersman and his Indian partner beyond it, yet he attributes to the couple the status of Adam and Eve, progenitors of a new form of humanity. Leslie Feidler agrees with Lawrence, denying the sexuality of the relations between nonwhite and white partners, but attributing their closeness to the status of heroes of nineteenth-century American culture. Their bonds are in part erotic, but without the constraints of sexual categories that limit thinking about sexuality today, Cooper described love stories between men that are erotic; they do not deploy the pejorative view of twentieth-century deviant sexual categories. Cooper does not skip thematizing and therefore mythologizing the sexual and erotic bonds between Chingachgook and Leatherstocking. Neither does he place his sailor-heroes beyond sex; rather, their relations include coded homoerotic bonds, connections that last their lifetimes and that sometimes produce biracial children.

While it would be inaccurate to say that Cooper's texts describe actual sex between his two most famous characters, homoeroticism encoded in words such as "fri'nd" and "fancy" suggest certain metaphors linking their intimacy to conjugal rituals. A careful look at *The Deerslayer, The Pioneers, The Pilot*, and *The Two Admirals* reveals a homoerotic core in the first myth about white masculinity in wilderness America. As Cooper's mythic characters disseminated into popular culture in the dime novels that were published between 1860 and 1890, the cowboy and Indian tale emerged as the nation's favorite formula tale. Writers borrowed Cooper's originals, reproducing not only their nonstop action and adventure in wilderness settings, but also reproducing the coded eroticism.

Of the five novels in *The Leatherstocking Tales, The Deerslayer* was written last, and it covers Nathaniel Bumppo's early years. Set in 1740 in the Finger Lakes region of upper New York State, the novel opens as the 18 year old journeys to meet his "fri'nd" Chingachgook, chief of the Delaware tribe, to join his warpath against the Huron who have kidnapped Chingachgook's fiancée. Bumppo is an eternally optimistic, youthful, and handsome fellow in buckskins, an excellent marksman, variously named young sapling Deerslayer, Hawkeye, and Leatherstocking. (In his elder years, he is called Pathfinder and Trapper.) His partner is a noble savage of titanic proportions, Chingachgook, or in English, "Big Sarpent," who is "so called for his wisdom and cunning . . . and prudence" (LT I 631).[4] Their relations are intimate, and their devotion to each other lasts a lifetime. While partnered, they share economic resources and food rations; they assist each other in warfare, defending territory and in *The Last of the Mohicans* even relinquishing it together. They raise two children together; they share living quarters. Theirs is a marriage, but what holds Leatherstocking and Chingachgook together is also radically different from a traditional marriage. Their bond does not require fidelity, for example.[5] (Chingachgook marries Wah-ta!-Wah and fathers a son while maintaining close ties with Deerslayer. When Wah-ta!-Wah dies, the two frontiersmen raise Uncas, the last Mohican, together.) Their bond does not presuppose gender-based dichotomies in divisions of labor, domestic duties, or economic roles.

As a youth, Deerslayer exhibits strong erotic interest in Chingachgook. "I love a just man, Sarpent," he says in just one of his eruptions of affection for his partner. "His eyes are never covered with darkness towards his inimies, while they are all sunshine and brightness towards his fri'nds" (LT II 683). As the Delaware chief's only white "fri'nd," Deerslayer enjoys the brightness of Chingachgook's eyes when they are focused on him. He ignores the erotic appeals of women like Judith Hutter, the slatternly daughter of a pirate whom he must protect from enemies.

Under Judith's flirtatious scrutiny, Deerslayer is clearly nervous. "I'm here as Chingachgook's aid and helper," he explains to her, "and if we can get the young maiden he likes back ag'in, it will give me almost as much pleasure, as if I'd got back my own sweetheart." (LT II 616). When Judith asks where Deerslayer's sweetheart is, he gives a sentimental reply:

> She's in the forest, Judith—hanging from the boughs of the trees, in a soft rain—in the dew on the open grass—the clouds that float about in the blue heavens—the birds that sing in the woods—the sweet springs where I slake my thirst—and in all the other glorious gifts that come from God's Providence. (LT II 616–617)

Virginal, chaste, dewy, feminine: this version of nature is a far cry from the kind of wilderness Deerslayer traverses in all five *Leatherstocking Tales*, where craggy mountains, howling storms, searing deserts, raging rivers, thunderous stampedes, and deadly forest fires occupy the vast majority of nature descriptions. Even the style of Deerslayer's speech changes when he waxes rhapsodic over this feminine version of nature. The repeated use of the dash separating phrases, for example, is nowhere else typical of his stiff, formal speech patterns.

His claim that feminine nature is his sweetheart is so incongruous that Judith immediately sees his decoy and exposes the subtext of his answer: "You mean that—as yet—you've never loved one of my sex, but love best your haunts, and your own manner of life." Leatherstocking affirms her assumption ("That's it—that's just it," he replies), but he dissembles immediately following:

> I am white—have a white heart, and can't, in reason, love a red skinned maiden, who must have a red-skin heart, and feelin's. No—no—I'm sound enough, in them partic'lars, and hope to remain so, at least, 'till this war is over. I find my time too much taken up with Chingachgook's affair, to wish to have one of my own. (LT II 617)

Deerslayer's sudden swerve into a hesitant discourse on red-skinned maidens' hearts is a revealing deception covering over the unstated answer: having never loved a white woman, and facing the impossibility of loving a "red-skinned maiden" because of the implied unsoundness of miscegenation, Bumppo finds it easiest to devote himself to a handsome young warrior named Chingachgook, whose affair with Wah-ta!-Wah is a displaced but permissible reproduction of his own suppressed desire. Since his feminine "sweetheart" nature is not a believable option, and his redskin maiden represents a prohibited desire, then desiring what Chingachgook desires is the only available path for him. He wants a squaw but accepts a male substitute. Here is the nexus of the way desire is constructed in *The Pioneers*: Deerslayer wants what Chingachgook wants, but since he fears the reproductive consequences, he shifts his desire to his "fri'nd." Aiding the Delaware chief's desire is enough for Deerslayer. Their "fri'ndship" implies erotic feelings and wished-for sexual practices, the same practices that produce children when one of the partners is female.

"[A]ll things that touches a fri'nd consarn a fri'nd" (LT I 616) announces Leatherstocking, and in the wilderness, where no law but the survival of the fittest governs behavior, this mythical white man's fantasy, tainted with the racist ideology of the 1820s, eroticizes this "fri'ndship."[6] Cooper's vision of the erotic relations between the two woodsmen is decidedly racist and sexist if judged by today's standards. Moreover, it is elitist in terms of class privilege. Leatherstocking is a veritable poster boy for the Manifest Destiny doctrines of the Jacksonian period, and his relation to Chingachgook functions in the way Lawrence and Feidler suspect; mythically.

Any study of empire looks to its literature for dramatization of its ideologies, and those found in Cooper's *Leatherstocking Tales* promote an inevitable Anglo supremacy over non-Anglo cultures and peoples in North America. Traditionally, Leatherstocking has been seen as an interloper from the white world, a harbinger, a warning of conquerors to follow, but not necessarily a conqueror himself.[7] Leatherstocking rejects the "wasty ways" of his fellow Anglo-Americans, and he seems to feel the presumed privileges of his race as a burden. (I use the term "race" in its nineteenth-century definition by white elites throughout this chapter because it is the definition that Cooper used.)

Therefore, at the center of this myth about inevitable white inheritance of lands is a hybrid figure that resists the Manifest Destiny doctrine while upholding its inevitability. "I'm white in blood," Deerslayer declares, "though a little red skin in feelings and habits." As a threshold figure, he eschews intimate relations with white women because he rejects perpetuating a race he disapproves of, and he can't satisfy his desire for red skin women because he fears the unsoundness of cross-racial reproduction. The only person who can receive his erotic desires is Chingachgook, through the faculty of his imagination. Cooper essentially creates a fantasy of the ideal friendship, where all his needs for companionship serve his own interests. Eroticizing relations with his "fri'nd" serves to legitimate their privileged status in the wilderness, to create the kinship ties that assist Deerslayer's survival. Cooper's solution to the problem of Deerslayer's desire is to turn it toward, but not beyond, Chingachgook.

The word "fri'nd" describes a cluster of intimate relations that includes erotic transference. The word "fancy" also includes erotic meanings in Cooper's vocabulary. For example, Bumppo greets his " 'arliest and latest fri'nd" with a hearty laugh, "excited more perhaps by the delight of having got his friend safe at his side, under circumstances so trying, than by any conceit that happened to cross his fancy" (LT II 631). His delight is primarily the product of relief at having escaped, safely, from a near-death situation, and secondarily the result of a "conceit" that may have crossed his "fancy." I'd like to focus upon this secondary meaning, for it has specific significance in the vocabulary of *The Deerslayer*. In the first chapter, Harry March, the handsome, boisterous trapper who accompanies Bumppo on his way to his reunion with Chingachgook, defines "fancy" as an involuntary desire for a beautiful woman, the very Judith Hutter whose flirtation Deerslayer will reject later. Deerslayer's lack of interest in Harry's "fancy" for Judith causes the hunter to reject the youth as a pre-pubescent know-nothing, "a sapling who has scarce got root," but Deerslayer's root, we shall see, is quite well dug into his desire, but only when it comes to Native American sexual discourses.

Elsewhere we are told that Deerslayer "is not adept in the mysteries of Cupid" (LT I 716), but the illiterate backwoodsman is highly adept at the way "fancy" works among the Delaware Indians: "Chingachgook is a comely Injin, and is much look'd upon and admired by the young women of this tribe, both on account of his family, and on account of himself." With high economic status, good ancestry, and admirable physical comliness, the Great Sarpent is worth the "fancy" he inspires in women of his tribe. Wah-ta!-Wah, the "darter" of another Delaware chief, is "the one most sought a'ter and craved for a wife, by all the young warriors of the nation." Outlining a system that at first glance resembles the middle-class Anglo-American concerns of marrying well, Deerslayer describes how "he fancied *her*, and she fancied *him*," and once the tribal elders approve, this fancy leads to cohabitation and sex, as evidenced by the birth of a child (LT II 616). However, Deerslayer also understands how a rival suitor for Wah-ta!-Wah's affection would become Chingachgook's enemy, and he suspects this motive in the sudden kidnapping of Wah-ta!-Wah by "inimies" of the tribe. In other words, Deerslayer is conversant in the sexual discourses of Native Americans, but he is ignorant about the code of conduct associated with Cupid's arrow. His allegiance is clear, so when he does feel "fancy" for Chingachgook, it is the Indian kind.

When Deerslayer erupts with delight upon seeing Chingachgook safe and sound, a conceit crosses his fancy. If the verb *to fancy* includes a meaning of *to desire sexually* in *The Deerslayer*, then what is conceit? It is essentially an impulsive, fleeting, and erotic appreciation of Chingachgook's near-naked body. Forty years after the event, Deerslayer fondly remembers his delight upon reuniting with Chingachgook in the woods that day. He tells his adopted grandson that Chingachgook, now 80 and decrepit, was "as comely a red-skin as ye ever set eyes on." He remembers first catching sight of Chingachgook in those woods: "He was naked, all to his breech-cloth and leggens; and you never seed a creater so handsomely painted" (LT I 155). His adopted grandson listens raptly as the wise old Leatherstocking describes his impressions; he is teaching his grandson how to admire the image of a near-naked savage in the woods.

It is worth dwelling briefly on the white male fascination with Native American nakedness in wilderness settings, for such descriptions are ubiquitous in literature about encounters between Anglos and Indians. From Puritan accounts before 1800, to reports from the Indian Wars of the pre-1850 period, to the exploration of the South Sea islands of the late nineteenth century, Anglo-American interest in, and clucking disapproval of, the unashamed nakedness and affections of "savages" is high. To the mind of a nineteenth-century white American, such a figure implies pagan excesses, unrestrained impulses, immoderate desire, and of course sex without limit.[8] In the following passage from Francis Parkman's *The Oregon Trail* (1845), the observer's erotic interest in the naked bodies of Ogallala [Sioux spelling] warriors is obscured by his reference to sculptural forms in Rome:

> Others again stood carelessly among the throng, with nothing to conceal the matchless symmetry of their forms; and I do not exaggerate when I say, that only on the prairie and in the Vatican have I seen such faultless models of the human figure. See that warrior standing by the tree, towering six feet and a half in stature. Your eyes trace the whole of his graceful and majestic height, and discover no defect or blemish. (144)

Parkman's comparison of an Ogallala warrior to statues in the Vatican allows admiration of symmetry, beauty, and form, but conceals the prurient interest in its subject.[9] As the observer's address shifts from the first person "I" to the second person "you," he first creates a framework that he then compels readers to use in order to properly appreciate the bodies. "Use your imagination," Parkman seems to say, "to scour the body for defects, where you'll find none." Parkman uses standard Enlightenment reasoning in rewriting the warrior's bodies as artistically perfect, a rationale that Rousseau used in asserting his famous dichotomy between the "natural man"—a pure, good, amoral creature driven by instinct and lacking imagination—and the "civilized man"—who is not pure, who is controlled by morals, who adheres to justice and abides by reason, who is divorced from nature but endowed with the privilege of imagination and therefore entitled to dominate the natural man. Imagination, then, is a quality reserved for Europeans and their descendants in the colonies, and it lends an advantage over aboriginals. "By the imagination," writes Adam Smith,

> we place ourselves in [another's] situation, we conceive ourselves enduring all the same torments, we enter as it were into his body, and become in some measure the same person with him, and thence form some idea of his sensations, and even feel something which, though weaker in degree, is not altogether unlike them.

Whatever passions, pleasures, or pain an individual feels, Smith and other Enlightenment philosophers proposed that the elite white men can exercise through their sympathy and imagination a "moral sense" (an actual organ in the body) that is responsible for the "fellow-feeling" between men, which is a universal human quality that is the cornerstone of harmonious communities. This privilege permits "civilized" men to exercise authority over Native Americans, who lack the imaginative faculty and therefore cannot presume to know another's experience.

When Chingachgook "disencumber[s] himself of his civilized garb," taking off a white man's disguise, and "stands forth an Indian warrior again," he reveals himself to Deerslayer's admiring eyes as "a son of the wilderness." Deerslayer watches the handsome chief walk "out on the platform in his scanty attire, an Apollo of the wilderness." What does the chief think as he gazes at the lakeshore where his betrothed is held captive? Deerslayer, with his sympathetic ability to imagine Chingachgook's situation, attributes to him "a hundred of the tender fancies that fleet through lovers' brains" (716). Here is fancy. Here is desire, exercised through the image-producing sense organ, creating the "fellow feeling" so essential to human bonds. Because he rejects white women and Indian squaws as objects of desire, Deerslayer participates in erotic discourse vicariously through Chingachgook. Only by watching, admiring, and essentially shadowing this nearly nude son of the wilderness can Deerslayer participate in the impulsive passions of nature.

The wilderness is where Deerslayer and Chingachgook function with almost telepathic unity. In the woods and on the warpath together, "both had all their feelings of pride and manhood enlisted in their success" (LT II 754–755). Such investments of feeling by two young warriors devoted to the same cause, according to Deerslayer, is like an invisible string, one end of which "is fast to the heart of . . . Chingachgook," and the other end of which is tied to Deerslayer's heart: "He has come here, led by the string, and I've followed, or rather come afore, for I got here first, pulled by nothing stronger than fri'ndship" (LST II 777). When two hearts are forever linked through an invisible string called "fri'ndship," no matter where in the wilderness they are, they must obey. This unspoken bond of erotic love is a cornerstone of the masculine code in frontier contexts. This is the source of their mutual loyalty: a string that unites their two destinies in the woods into one. This unbreakable string explains their 40-year "fri'ndship." Looking at their final years together, it is difficult to find the erotic spark that lights up Chingachgook's eyes or causes Deerslayer to feel an impulsive surge of delight upon seeing his naked "fri'nd" in the woods. Instead, they affirm their bond through parenthood, adopting Oliver Edwards, a young half-breed, who lives with them in their remote cabin. Part Delaware, descended from a chief, and part white (he never specifies a mother), Edwards is an adopted grandson and his mixed blood is a signifier in bodily form of the erotic bond that Leatherstocking and Chingachgook share.

The Pioneers is set in the 1780s, just after the American Revolution. Both the warriors are now old men, living in an "Indian style" cabin near Lake Otsego. The recent arrival of white settlers has disrupted their sylvan seclusion. The settlers are very curious about the all-male multiracial family that lives in this cabin; they seek to know the secrets of the cabin in order to normalize it. Particularly the young women of the settlement want to know how the handsome young bachelor came to live in Old John Mohegan's and Leatherstocking's cabin, and who his parents are. (In *The Pioneers*, Chingachgook is called Mohegan and Deerslayer is called Leatherstocking.) Persistent questioning of this bristly youth reveals that in spite of his veneer of educated speech and good manners, and in spite of his claim to have been baptized, his grandfather was a Delaware chief named Young Eagle. He is therefore a mixed-breed individual and is not eligible to marry into the elite classes.

According to town gossip, Oliver Edwards's mixed races prevent him from practicing the "turn-the-other-cheek" philosophy of the Episcopalian settlers. His hot temper, bravery, dark good looks, and first-rate intellect make him one of Cooper's classic heroes—an unavailable romantic figure with glossy curls, a passionate defender of democracy, and a symbol of

Illustration 4 Classic westerns insisted that the typical cowboy of the Old West was Anglo-American, but research in the 1960s revealed that up to 40 percent of cattle workers were African American, and an untold percentage were Mestizo Americans. Ungrounded assumptions about the cowboy's sexual abstinence while riding the range should be similarly questioned. Three cowboys with cards and liquor, n.d. Photographer unknown. Kansas Collection, The University of Kansas Libraries, accession number RH PH 26.32.

future leadership in America. When one of his anti-wealth diatribes frightens a young lady, her father explains disapprovingly, "It is the hereditary violence of a natives' passion" that prevents this half-breed from succeeding in polite society (LT I 143).

Edwards's parentage is of particular interest to Elizabeth Temple because she has fallen in love with him, and her wealthy landowner father, Judge Temple, won't permit a marriage. As the son of a queer interracial partnership, Edwards is aligned with two former warriors whose occupation of the land predates Judge Temple's ownership of it. Edwards is therefore a double threat to both civic law and well as the presumed natural law governing racial purity. According to the pastor, "[N]either the refinements of education nor the refinements of our excellent liturgy, have been able entirely to eradicate the evil" (LT I 143) in Edwards. Blood is blood, say the white settlers, but Elizabeth believes she can eradicate Edwards's Indian blood, and Cooper grants her wish through a highly implausible dues-ex-machina plot twist that reverses Edwards's queer interracial family history as well as his Indian blood, transforming him into a racially pure Anglo-American of the elite class.

Edwards loses his Indian half in the penultimate chapter, when the secret of Mohegan's and Leatherstocking's cabin is finally revealed: Edwards's grandfather, the legendary Young Eagle, has been living with them, but to the amazement of the townspeople, he is white. He is now a decrepit old man (by my count he would be about 150 years old) with snow-white locks who can't even speak for himself (444). His grandson explains a complicated patrimonial genealogy that proves not only his own racial purity, but also his hereditary co-entitlement to the lands owned by Judge Temple. All in a moment, the former half-breed, hot-tempered son of the queer wilderness becomes a descendent of Major Effingham, a wealthy land baron, and a suitable match for Elizabeth Temple. Edwards declares, "I have no other Indian blood or breeding; though I have seen the hour, Judge Temple, when I could wish that such had been my lineage and education" (LT I 449). By relinquishing his claim to be of Delaware descent, Edwards reduces his experiences in the woods to a memory, aligning himself with the white elite Americans. Judge Temple offers his daughter's hand in marriage, and the house of Leatherstocking unites with the Temples, restoring Anglo-American legitimacy at the expense of wilderness and the aboriginals who inhabit it. Edwards's transformation from queer to elite ensures a future of wealthy American-born, racially pure sons whose erased queer parentage and biracial identity entitle them to own the wilderness.

In *The Leatherstocking Tales*, the Anglo-American frontiersman and the Delaware chief function as the nexus for all encounters between whites and Indians. They raise an adopted son, whose skills in the wilderness match his grandfathers' skills, but who abandons the wilderness to lead the first waves of white settlers advancing westward into the territories from the United States. The parental partnership between Leatherstocking and Chingachgook, two racially different but spiritually harmonious bachelors, produces leaders of an emerging democracy, who function equally well in the wilderness or in the drawing room: Oliver Edwards in *The Pioneers*. Cooper invents similar hybridized characters in two of his sea tales: Harry Wilder in *The Red Rover*, and Tom Wycherly in *The Two Admirals*. All are foundlings, raised by their respective interracial hero-lover dads in the woods or aboard ships, all of whom turn out to be high-born aristocrats whose biracial lineage was a mistake or a masquerade. Transformed from hybrid half-savages of queer parentage to elite white men of aristocratic lineage, these sons of frontiersmen signal the end of wilderness in North America. According to the racist ideology of the Manifest Destiny doctrines, the Indian inevitably passes from the stage of evolutionary history, while "new humanity" of Anglo-American masculinity rises to dominance, built upon an erased, then re-imagined foundation of intimate bonds with aboriginals. Cooper's novels illustrate these doctrines.

In *The Red Rover*, Dick Fid and Scipio Africanus, one a Yankee whale man and the other a brawny seagoing African, enjoy a lifelong partnership that started when they survived a shipwreck, and was cemented when they found an infant and agreed to raise it together. Their adopted son is named Harry Wilder, an appropriate metonym for a young man raised outside the sphere of civilization. Like Oliver Edwards in *The Pioneers*, Wilder is mistaken to be a half-breed. Wilder's skin has accumulated "tinges of brown, which had been laid on his features, layer after layer, in such a constant succession, as to have changed to a deep olive, a complexion which had once been fair, through which the rich blood was still mantling with the finest glow of vigorous health."[10] With his manly features and intellectual head, his mass of black ringlet hair and his stocky build, Wilder is a classic of Cooper's romantic sailor-heroes, with racially ambiguous skin tones.

Wilder, like Edwards in *The Pioneers*, is a hot-blooded hero, moody and volatile, capable of perceiving reason but just as prone to impulsive passion. Just as Edwards is an expert backwoodsman, Wilder is a lithe and skilled sailor, and a capable leader of men. Like Edwards, Wilder is not really a half-breed: a coincidence at the end of *The Red Rover* proves Wilder's aristocratic ancestry just in time for him to marry an eligible wealthy woman. Both these characters, upon proving themselves successful boundary-crossers, shed their status as half-breeds and are transformed aristocrats and leaders of the new American nation.

Their fathers, however, remain outcasts, committed to their partners, seeking wilderness where their relationships are not subject to the censure of the Anglo-American world. Dick Fid is a corollary figure to Deerslayer, but he is far less circumspect than the uptight frontiersman. He is a "worthy minister of Bacchus," according to his barroom buddies. In Boston he shares a wife with four other seamen, none of whom are in port at the same time. He is a grizzled and lusty mariner from the American colonies, given to telling tall tales and salting his language with burlesques. When it comes to his queer family, however, his jesting turns to candor: "I fell in with the Guinea," he says, and "I care not who knows it, after Master Harry there is no man living who has an honester way with him, or in whose company I take greater satisfaction" (755). Fid and Africanus have been together so long, says Fid, that "the colour has got into my eyes, and now it suits as well as another" (489), and he loves him in spite of his skin that is "no whiter than the back of a whale." In fact, Cooper seems to go out of his way to mix racial taxonomies between this long-term couple. With his low forehead, "nearly covered with hair," his small eyes, and his obstinate nose, Fid is strongly associated with the phrenological types of the lower classes. Here Cooper participates in the widespread characterization in the 1840s by Anglo-Americans of Irish Americans as base and vulgar. Africanus, on the other hand, has a face far more open and joyous than his white partner's; in the racist terms of Cooper's novel, he is "not as hideous as some of his race," with elevated features, a mild eye, and a simpleton's enjoyment of natural phenomenon. His uncanny ability to read and interpret the weather, or the intentions of a distant ship from the arrangements of her rigging, classifies him as a familiar stereotype: the illiterate soothsayer whose superstitions are always accurate.[11]

In addition to his superior sense perceptions, Africanus has an arm that "might have served as a model for the limb of Hercules" (ST 451). Both Fid, with the black in his eye and upon his face, and Africanus, with his pre-Herculean arm, have inculcated cultural references from each other's physical and cultural genealogy, generating hybrid forms: Anglo males in semi-marriage arrangements with non-Anglo males, each imbibing and eventually staining his original racial purity to the point where he resembles his partner. Their sons, too, absorb racial otherness in layer after layer of color and "fellow-feeling" for savages and outcasts.

Here Cooper's model of hybridism, of uniting difference within couples, promotes an exchange of race and culture through intimacies that, were the partners of opposite sexes, would imply sexual practices and reproductive consequences. When the two partners are male, Cooper avoids the problem of miscegenation but still explores the possibilities of cultural exchange through intimate, and erotic, relations between representatives of each race. In this regard, American literary heroes in Cooper's myth differ from the hero-lover models of Antiquity: Achilles and Patroclus, whose promise to mix their ashes after death is so poignant in the *Iliad*; or Damian and Pythias, whose to-the-death loyalty so impresses a tyrant that he abandons tyranny; or Alexander the Great and his lifelong slave–warrior–lover Hephaestion. These friendships are central to the Greek concept of ideal love. Their love for each other, according to Aristophanes, is an example that ought to guide the learning of Greek youth, for it is the very type that exemplifies the ideal love of citizen for his nation.

Cooper adds an American twist to the Greek myths about their most celebrated men: instead of implying harmonious twins in the Hellenic model, he describes bonds built on difference, particularly racial difference. Still, these friendships are held up as models from which citizens ought to learn. The heroes in Cooper's American tales about origins are ideals. They form lifelong partnerships based on same-sex love; this love does not function by mirroring the Other but by exchanging difference and inculcating the Other into the Self.

A tattoo on Fid's bicep, inked there over 24 years ago by Africanus, shows two crossed anchors and the words "Ark of Lynnhaven." The two crossed anchors signify the two lost ships from which Africanus saved Fid when they first met, a symbol written on Fid's skin that commemorates when their friendship turned into a lifelong partnership. Their relationship goes beyond being temporary berth-buddies, or wives periodically visited when the ship is in port. It is a marriage, and Fid clings to it even after Africanus dies, when Fid proclaims perpetual fidelity: "I won't be berthing myself again, in any other man's hammock" (753). The Ark of Lynnhaven is the name of the second wrecked ship where Fid and Africanus found their infant son. With blackness in his eye, and intersecting anchors tattooed upon his arm, and his adopted son's pedigree inked around it, Fid is clearly committed to hybridism, and his charming statements of devotion to Africanus endow the pirate culture aboard the ship in *The Red Rover* with a spicy mix of irreverence, heroism, and *bonne homme* spirit. Like second-tier figures in a Shakespearean tragedy, humorous but flat, Fid's and Africanus's relationship serves as a foil to the main characters in the drama, namely Wilder and the Red Rover himself.

A similar pair appears on the sidelines of *The Pilot* (1823), Cooper's first sea tale. Captain Manual and Captain Borroughcliffe are not racially opposed, but are officers on opposing sides of a political crisis in Britain. Their drunken and foppish arguments punctuate with burlesque humor the otherwise serious conflict, and their sentimental apologies are genuinely loving. After years of jovial antagonism, including one duel, the two wind up living together in a remote cabin deep in the North American wilderness:

> [T]he intercourse between these worthies was renewed with remarkable gusto and at length arrived to so regular a pass that a log cabin was erected on one of the islands in the river, as a sort of neutral territory, where their feastings and revels might be held without any scandal to the discipline of their respective garrisons. (417)

That Cooper uses the word "intercourse" in a sentence where a log cabin gets erected for these two as a refuge in a wilderness setting, where feasting, revelry, and scandal occur, is probably no accident, since the word *intercourse* had a sexual meaning that he would have known about.[12]

The Pilot ends by lingering over the grave where Manual and Borroughcliffe are buried together—along with a casket of legendary Madeira wine. The narrator justifies this ending as utilitarian. Since "no widows and orphans were left to lament their separate ends," only novelists can commemorate lifelong erotic friendships like theirs (419). Cooper spent a good deal of time chronicling the male–male partnerships in the wilderness. Unlike twenty-first-century readers, he did not have a nuanced view of the differences between friendship and eroticism.

In another novel about a lifelong friendship between two sailors, Cooper chronicles the devotion that leads to a deathbed kiss and farewell in the tradition of Achilles and Patroclus, although he grudgingly acknowledges a bit of Romeo and Juliet. In the preface of *The Two Admirals*, Cooper writes,

> We hope the reader will do us the justice to regard the TWO ADMIRALS as a *sea*-story, and not as a *love* story. Our admirals are our heroes, and, as there are two of them, those who are particularly fastidious on such subjects, are quite welcome to term one the heroine, if they see fit. (TTA 5)

Cooper's flat joke implies that "fastidious" readers—by which he probably means feminine readers—might enjoy the "*love* story" between the two admirals, since they are a pair. Switching one of the Admirals from a hero to a heroine might help "fastidious" readers follow the plot. Less fastidious readers, probably masculine, will follow the action-packed "*sea* tale," and thus perceive the couple as heroes whose story about love is less important than the sea story.

Today let us be fastidious readers, concerned just with the love stories in Cooper's oeuvre. Consider this scene, in which the two admirals kiss for the last time.

> "Kiss me, Oakes," murmured the rear admiral.
>
> In order to do this, the commander in chief rose from his knees and bent over the body of his friend. As he raised himself from the cheek he had saluted, a benignant smile gleamed on the face of the dying man, and he ceased to breathe. (TTA 441–442)

With this kiss, with this smile, and with this death, Vice Admiral Sir Gervaise Oakes loses his lifelong companion and friend, Rear Admiral Richard Bluewater, his alter ego and bosom buddy. With the same instinctual connections shared by Deerslayer and Chingachgook, the two admirals triumphed over adversaries until a deathbed kiss divides them. While they are not racially different by nineteenth-century standards, they occupy opposite political loyalties, and their personalities clash.[13] Some would call this final goodbye scene turgid, sentimental, and the claim would have merit if measured by today's standards, but the fictional kiss derives from a factual deathbed kiss, famous in sailor lore, between Horatio Nelson and Lord Collingwood, two of the British Royal Navy's best, upon the demise of the former.[14] The demands of realism, therefore, require this kiss. The fictional construction of their emotional intimacy is all Cooper's.[15]

Is the last kiss between the two admirals erotic? I argue that insofar as kisses between warrior-heroes like David and Jonathan, Achilles and Patroclus, or Damian and Pythias honor Eros as well as Mars, then so too do the gestures of affection between the two admirals imply erotic and sexual practices as well as nonsexual affection. Cooper himself instructs readers to choose between reading *The Two Admirals* as a "love" story or as a "sea" story.[16]

According to an 1842 review of *The Two Admirals*, the relationship between Dick and Oakes is "a picture of friendship, almost approaching fraternal love . . . that melts the heart and sanctifies the connexion."[17] What this reviewer calls "fraternal love" causes a sentimental effect; it melts the universal heart and justifies itself in terms of religious sanctity. These terms refer to the privilege granted to good friends, whose trust and sympathy entitle them to leadership positions. At least half of *The Two Admirals* is devoted to resolving the Wycherly family's inheritance dilemma, a complicated subplot involving a long-lost nephew from America, an illegitimate son, and a mistaken-at-birth daughter. With the Wycherly family blood feud standing in as a simulacrum for the crisis of kingship informing the cross-Channel naval wars, Dick and Oakes, the two admirals, preside over family warfare and the national warfare in unassailable patriarchal privilege.

Whether occupying positions of secondary or primary status, Cooper's queer all-male families must necessarily go the way of the Indian. Deerslayer moves West after Chingachgook dies; Fid commits himself to the sea and to Africanus's memory upon the demise of his partner; the captains

Manual and Borroughcliffe lie buried in each other's arms, along with a case of wine. Bluewater and Oakes leave their legacy to their adopted American son before relinquishing their mortal coils. Cooper essentially assigns himself the task of first depicting the relations between two men as erotic, then giving this intimate couple a son, whose erased biracial identity helps him succeed in a new democracy. Cooper invents an American myth about nonnormative families that are bound at least in part by the erotic friendship between the two parental figures, whose relations provide an incubator for national heroes. Only in novels do we see the erased eroticism between male couples behind the great leaders of the emerging American nation.[18]

Cooper's influence, as I said at the beginning of this chapter, is difficult to overstate. The entire dime novel industry relied upon his formula to churn out thousands of paperbacks that were read by literally millions of Americans and immigrants during the 1860s to about 1880. Dime novel authors and writers of popular Westerns avoided Cooper's essayistic social histories and got right to the chase: near-constant adventures, crises, threats, all set in the American wilderness. Westerns were by far the most popular form of frontier adventure tales in the years following the Civil War. Drenched with the "blood and thunder" of man-to-man conflicts, varied only by man-against-nature conflicts, this popular form of literature borrowed not only from Cooper's penchant for describing violent conflict in wilderness conditions, but also Cooper's coded bonds between partners. Popular novelists invented all manner of blood-brother rituals to signify these bonds, some of them highly erotic.

Consider for example, the friendship between Charley and Captain Dick in *Live Boys; or, Charley and Nasho in Texas*, published in 1868. Captain Dick is a high-spirited, handsome trail-boss in his early twenties, and Charley is a teenage novice who has just joined his cowboy outfit. Their relationship is intimate: for example, after some of the rougher cowboys threaten Charley, Captain Dick insists that he sleep in his room. Charley confesses he was glad to have a room with him "because I liked him better than any of the others I saw."

One predicament Charley gets himself into when Captain Dick sends him out hunting is to wind up naked in a swampy wilderness with just a Bowie knife and the carcasses of two young bucks and a pair of swans. "That rascally Monkey,"[19] he says of his horse, had "run off" with all his clothes "and Nasho was after him." Abandoned by his Kickapoo partner and his horse, naked, with the sun dipping below the horizon and a cold wind blowing, Charley faces a crisis. Thanks to Nasho he has learned how to survive in the wilderness, so he quickly starts to work:

> I skinned the deer as fast as I could. Then I put one skin round each leg and fastened them with strings . . . round my waist to keep them up. Now I wanted a coat. I pitched into the swans, and cut the bellies, and found I could peel their skins, feathers and all, off just like the deer hides, only a heap easier . . . [They] made me a pretty good cloak, plenty big enough to go round me and cover me from the neck down below my waist. (178)

His transformation suggests a centaur as well as a swan maiden or possibly a Pegasus. Cloaked in swanskin and buckskin, he walks out of the swamp, intending to make it all the way back to the ranch house. Along the way, Charley discards the centaur costume but keeps the swan: "My cloak did first rate, but my leggins was rough and rubbed my legs and made it hard for me to travel" (179). When a rainsquall forces him to look for a campsite, he finds a stand of live oaks where he builds himself a nest out of "the finest, softest, dryest grass I could find, covering it with a lean-to. . . . [It] made me a snug place to lie down in" (179–180). Starting a fire without matches, he cooks up a linguistic hybrid of animals, a "venison ham" he'd cut from the deer. With his survivalist instincts satisfied, the young swan-boy grows sad, scared, and homesick, but he consoles himself by thinking of the men he loves most: Nasho, his Mestizo partner, and Captain Dick, his trail boss. Feeling better, he puts out his fire, nestles down, and sleeps.

I'd like to leave the swan-boy asleep in his nest for a moment while considering his butchery and then donning of the animal carcasses. On a practical level, Charley demonstrates that he has learned how to survive with very few resources. Nasho has taught him the ways of his people well. But on a symbolic level, he has literally become a hybrid human and swan. Like all the tribes of the Plains Indians, the Kickapoos believed that a young brave learns of his destiny as a man in a divinely inspired dream. Charley's swamp transformation and nest building suggest just such a dream, giving a clue to the man he is becoming.[20] He discards the buckskin and keeps the swan's cloak. Choices like these, in spiritual matters, are telling.

The swan in Kickapoo mythology is an important figure as it is in all Mid- and Southern-Plains tribes, as Barbara Fass Leavy outlines in *The Legend of the Swan Maiden*.[21] With a great many variations, the legend generally casts the swan as a supernatural bride who is captured by a mortal hunter using magic arrows. After a sequence of tests to see if the hunter is worthy, the swan uncloaks herself, takes human form, and offers herself as a reward-bride. The story is generative and signifies a revitalizing of the tribe, creating a new order after rejecting the old (103). Certain features of the legend echo Charley's transformed swan-boy story. For example, the hunter chases the swan into the setting sun, which is where Captain Dick comes looking for Charley. In most versions, the swan maiden signals her willingness to be captured by placing a "small torch" next to her wigwam fire. If the swan extinguishes the fire, she is receptive to the hunter's approach. If the fire burns, his visit is not welcome (Leavy 108). Charley, remember, puts out his fire before sleeping.

When Captain Dick finds Charley in his nest, he wakes him up. They embrace, and Captain Dick erupts emotionally, declaring, "when I [heard] you was stark naked six miles off, with no clothes or anyway to make fire . . . I struck out lively." Charley is overjoyed to see Captain Dick. "We was sitting down, . . . and he put his arm around me so I 'most felt like crying, for he seemed like an older brother, and you know I never had a brother. . . . And he drew me up in his arms on his breast, and I believe I cried a little. I do love Capt. Dick. . . . I think Capt. Dick was 'most crying too, for he pushed me away and said—Get your duds on, little one, and we'll have some supper" (182).

If the marriage between swan and hunter signifies a future new tribe, and if Charley's transformation suggests an appropriation of Kickapoo legend, then marriage between Charley and Captain Dick is a generative tale like the kind I have outlined in Cooper's fiction. The costume change from swan feathers to cowboy duds signals the end of yet another adventure for Charley, and a return from the indigenous dream state to the cowboy way. Their embrace amounts to a commitment ceremony signifying a revitalization of a tribe, the establishment of a "new humanity" that promises a future of adventures together, always in a realm outside "civilization."

James Fennimore Cooper invented the frontiersman who served as the model for the American cowboy in literature. Over the five-novel span of *The Leatherstocking Tales*, Cooper's hero, Nathaniel Bumppo, never married a white woman, although he had several opportunities to do so, because his desires tended another way—toward Indians, specifically Chingachgook. Loyalty to his partner's desires prevented Bumppo from marrying and settling down with a family. In Cooper's hands, the queer partnership between opposites permits a breeding ground for the principled future leaders of expanding United States, whose Anglo-American privilege is preserved. Erased family ties to aboriginals absolves them of guilt for replacing Indians and the wilderness itself with Anglo-American families and cultivated farms.

Capitalizing on the popularity of Cooper's literary hero, hundreds of writers produced thousands of dime novels, half-dime novels, and penny rags during the 1860s–1890s. Westerns were the most popular of these pulp productions. In action-drenched pages, cowboy heroes reenacted Bumppo's plains adventures—stampedes, brushfires, or Indian attacks. Between adventures, writers followed Cooper's lead by sparing a few paragraphs to illustrate idealized intimacy between partners, such as the reunion scene between Charley and Captain Dick in *Live Boys*. Careful analysis of these intimacies suggests that homoerotic language and imagery are part of the friendships, and homoerotic affection undergirds the devotion between partners.

CHAPTER TWO

REHEARSING AND RIDICULING MARRIAGE IN *THE VIRGINIAN* AND OTHER ADVENTURE TALES

At the end of Owen Wister's cowboy classic *The Virginian*, after the horseman-hero kills the last of the cattle rustlers in a shoot-out, he finally marries Molly Wood, the feisty schoolmarm, whom he has courted and sassed for so long. He takes her on a spectacular horseback honeymoon near the Gran Tetons. They camp on an island in an idyllic mountain stream, and after much sensuous language suggesting a ritualistic deflowering, husband and wife spend an idle afternoon drowsing on a rock by the stream. Interrupting their nuptial, a "little wild animal" swims by, and emerges from the stream to roll and stretch in the sand. As the mink trots away, the Virginian forms a homoerotic parable out of his visit.

> "I am like that fellow," he said dreamily. "I have often done the same." And stretching slowly his arms and legs he lay full length upon his back, letting his head rest upon her. "If I could talk his animal talk, I could talk to him," he pursued. "And he would say to me: 'Come and roll on the sands. Where's the use of fretting? What's the gain in being a man? Come roll on the sands with me.' That's what he would say." (384)

The repeated invitations to "roll on the sands" and the pointed emphasis on translating "animal talk" suggest a playful alternative to the careworn world of husbands and their duty to uphold wifehood.[1] The Virginian does

Illustration 5 Left too long without women, cowboys get so "foxy," in the words of a bachelor-ranchman, "you couldn't bait him into a matrimonial trap with sweet grapes." Detail from "Outdoor sleeping arrangements at the W.D. Boice Cattle Company," photographer unknown. State Historical Society of Colorado Library accession number F14800 10029724/10026001.

not answer this call of the wild, but he nonetheless recognizes its appeal. As a married man, he must now fret about his wife and her domestic needs. He wishes Molly could forget he is "responsible." Often when he camped there alone, he tells her, he has wanted to

> "become the ground, become the water, become the trees, mix with the whole thing. Not know myself from it. Never unmix again. Why is that?" he demanded, looking at her. "What is it? You don't know, nor I."[2]

The riddle vexes the backwoods philosopher. His desire to experience nature without differentiating himself from it is a fantasy worthy of Rousseau, who believed that savages had just such unselfconscious relationships with nature, while civilized men suffered self-awareness due to their more highly evolved moral sense. Cowboys are hybrid figures in this paradigm, with the animalistic habits and morals of natives, but crafty enough to make fools of city folks, lawmen, religious types, and aristocrats. They "mix" wholly with nature while in the wilderness, and scramble social law and religious conviction with a kind of burlesque glee while in town. Left too long in the arms of the wilderness, some cowboys could get so "foxy," in the words of a bachelor ranchman, "you couldn't bait him into a matrimonial trap with sweet grapes."[3] Because marrying Molly disqualifies the Virginian from the cowboy brotherhood altogether, his reluctance to give up his wild man fantasy is strong. His desire for a union with a wifeless wilderness lives on in his parable of the mink. His roistering years are over at the close of Wister's novel; he relinquishes his cowboy identity, and repudiates his views that wives, children, and Christians are anathema to the cowboy code.

"Come roll on the sands with me," calls the mink in his animal language—or so translates the Virginian for his new wife and readers of Wister's novel. Out of hearing of mixed company, the Virginian indulges in some plainspoken "elemental talk of sex" with his then-partner Steve:

> "For Steve and me most always hunted in couples back in them gamesome years," he explained. And he fell into the elemental talk of sex, such talk as would be an elk's or tiger's; and spoken so by him, simply and naturally, as we speak of the seasons, or of death, or of any actuality, it was without offence. But it would be offence should I repeat it. (322)

The "elemental talk of sex" cannot be spoken—or grunted—out loud in polite society because "it would be offence" to repeat it. No shame governs their sex talk; to the Virginian and Steve, it is like talking about the weather. The narrator, however, avoids offense by encoding it with metaphors of elk and tiger. Analysis of these avoidances suggests that the narrator is trying to tell a hidden story about cowboy culture, one that is about sex, men, the wilderness, and animal languages. Never named explicitly, always hinted at, the homoerotic contours of this motif suggest that cowboy desires function to exclude femininity and to preserve a privileged relationship to the wilderness and to each other. Namby-pamby euphemisms for sex in the language used by East Coast socialites is not interesting to the narrator, but each time the Virginian expresses some raunchy, males-only talk, the narrator practically wilts with the unspoken pleasures that wives enjoy.

From the very first page of *The Virginian*, marriage between men and women is the subject of derisive mockery, while homoerotic bonds reveal deeply held personal truths. When the narrator, then a prissy East Coast snob visiting Wyoming for the first time, spies "a slim young giant, more beautiful than pictures," he is overwhelmed by the physical appeal of this "ungrammatical son of the soil." When he overhears the Virginian making fun of an old cuss for proposing marriage to six different women, and being rejected six different times, the East Coast dandy archly comments, "Had I been the bride, I should have taken the giant, dust and all" (3). Later, when he catches a lusty smile on the Virginian's face, he speculates, "had I been a woman, it would have made me do what he please with on the spot" (195). The eagerly submissive narrator can easily imagine playing the woman's role in sex and marriage. His initial impression of the sexy cowboy focuses on his physique—"the undulations of a tiger, smooth and easy, as if all his muscles flowed beneath his skin" (2). Later, when he learns about the Virginian's mind, he falls in love with him, and they become intimate comrades. As much as *The Virginian* is about a cowboy giving up his occupation to marry the schoolmarm, it is also about the increasingly intimate friendship between the narrator and the Virginian.

Thinking about what a bride would do to the Virginian's tiger-like body, "dust and all," the narrator is thrilled to learn that his fantasy husband will be his personal wilderness guide during his visit, and a friendship will develop in future visits that is as close as, and perhaps closer than, the intimacy between husband and wife. The combination of brawn, beauty, and untutored philosophy in one man makes the narrator desire more than just companionship; he wants to marry this cowboy in all senses of the word. *The Virginian* is the narrator's sometimes-erotic homage to this cowboy, a 400-page love letter chronicling the years before the Virginian quits his roguish ways and marries the schoolmarm.

While waiting for the narrator's bags at the train depot, the Virginian meets his former roistering partner, Steve, and the two indulge in some more linguistic trickery that hints at unspoken homoeroticism. They begin speaking in a code that to the greenhorn narrator is indecipherable. Calling it a "speech of the fourth dimension," the narrator is dimly aware of the two cowboys mocking him; but not as yet having learned the code, he cannot translate their meaning:

> "Your first visit to this country?"
> I told him yes.
> "How do you like it?"
> I expected to like it very much.
> "How does the climate strike you?"
> I thought the climate was fine.
> "Makes a man thirsty, though."
> This was the sub-current which the Virginian plainly looked for. But he, like Steve, addressed himself to me.
> "Yes," he put in, "thirsty while a man's soft yet. You'll harden."
> "I guess you'll find it a drier country than you were given to expect," said Steve.
> "If your habits have been frequent that way," said the Virginian.
> "There's parts of Wyoming," pursued Steve, "where you'll go hours and hours before you'll see a drop of wetness."
> "And if yu' keep a-thinkin' about it," said the Virginian, "it'll seem like days and days."
> Steve, at this stroke, gave up and clapped him on the shoulder with a joyous chuckle. (18–19)

Kicking the "you" pronoun back and forth, the Virginian and Steve use the inept narrator as a foil for their humorous discourse about thirst and hardness, which in their lexicon appears to mean tolerance for being parched. But being hard, for men in the West, also means wanting, thirsting, but not getting wetness. Affection, joy, and intimacy are the result of the "subcurrent" of their private meaning. The two cowboys exclude the greenhorn from the code, but they make sure he knows he has been insulted. The narrator, fresh off the train from the States, is soft, wet, thirsty—and utterly clueless. "Clearly this wild country spoke a language other than mine," he remarks sardonically.

Eventually, the narrator learns to speak the language of the territory. His exposure to Wyoming's harsh and beautiful wilderness, and sartorial cowboys like the Virginian, hardens him. He replaces Steve as the Virginian's most intimate friend.[4] Not enough readers pay attention to the progress of this erotic friendship in *The Virginian*. The narrator's transformation from soft to hard is motivated by his erotic alliance with the Virginian. From their

Illustration 6 Gestures of casual intimacy between posing cowboys suggest the ease with which these communities of partnered men touch one another in ways that seem erotic today. Detail from "Occ.Cowboys" posing on a tree trunk, 1904 by C.A. Kendrick. Colorado Historical Society accession number F040330, 10025448.

first meeting, the narrator imagines himself as the Virginian's bride, and always strives to be close to the cowboy. The reward for such an alliance is status among an elite community. The dangers of such privileged closeness are equally apparent. "You have a friend," the Virginian explains to the narrator, "and his ways are your ways. You travel together, you spree together confidentially, and you suit each other down to the ground. Then one day you find him putting his iron on another man's calf" (310). Since Steve betrays their friendship this way, since Steve violates the "custom of the country" by rustling cattle instead of earning an honest cowboy's wages, the Virginian must kill him. The narrator, as Steve's replacement, learns the terms of male–male friendships in the "wild country" of the American West: homoerotic unity can turn to fratricide in the blink of an eye, if the cowboy code gets violated. The language of these fundamentally unifying or destructive practices is coded within the wilderness in which they occur.

REHEARSING AND RIDICULING MARRIAGE 47

Those who doubt that Wister intended to communicate underlying erotic currents in his fiction ought to know about his poem, penned in 1893 in his journal during a sojourn through Texas. It begins "There are some things we say but must not hear; / There are some things we do yet cannot know." Wister's poem on denial argues that subjects "unfit and shocking" should be in literature and art, but decorum demands "fig leaves" and "hymns" to cover them up. In the concluding stanza, he seems angry about the constraints of stuffy drawing room etiquette on representations of the naked human body:

> Yes, I'm aware your daughter cannot read it;
> I don't forget your piano stands on limbs.
> Life's so indelicate, we have agreed it
> Must be concealed by fig leaves and by hymns.
> Sculpture's so bare, and painting so illicit,
> And poets unconventional at best;
> Give Art a chance and Art will never miss it;
> Art has a craving to parade undressed.[5] (253–254)

Illustration 7 "To need no clothes" during an idylic campout in the Gran Tetons, "is better than purple and fine linens," according to a would be cowboy in *The Virginian*. Detail from "Cowboys Bathing in Pond," F.M. Steele. Kansas Historical Society accession number F596–27.

Wister draws literary principles rather starkly: truth is nakedness and art is truth. Lies are for delicate daughters and draped piano legs. The artist's task is to negotiate meaning so that the truth can be naked enough to be true, but disguised enough so that "daughters" can read it without being offended. Like ostriches, Wister says, readers often bury their heads in print "so that none shall see / Your large wise body looming through the sham."

Wister shows the Virginian's large, wise, naked body, and the narrator's adoration of it, during a camping trip, deep in the wilderness.[6] It is the second summer of their acquaintance. The Virginian is currently jobless, "drifting," and he had written to the narrator in New York suggesting they go on an elk hunting trip together (396). They meet at the juncture of the Buffalo and Snake rivers, an extremely remote region between the Gran Tetons and the Rockies, in an area then newly named Yellowstone National Park.

They camp on an island in the Snake River. On a drowsy afternoon spent casting for fish, the narrator can tell something is bothering his friend, but he knows enough not to question him. "Have you ever studied much about marriage?" the cowboy asks abruptly, introducing the theme he will discuss for the next several pages. The narrator says no.

> "Let's swim," suggests the Virginian, since the fish aren't biting.
>
> Forthwith we shook off our boots and dropped our few clothes and heedless of what fish we might now drive away, we went into the cool, slow, deep breadth of backwater which the bend makes just there. As he came up near me, shaking his head of black hair, the cow-puncher was smiling a little. (396)

Their wilderness skinny-dipping might seem nonerotic, the black-haired horseman's little smile might seem just friendly, but the narrator's line-up of adjectives—"cool, slow, deep"—and romantic phrasing of "just there" in naming the bend in the river, hints at a mood of intimacy. Hungry to know what the Virginian wants to say about marriage, but a novice in reading his mind, the narrator "looked at the Southerner, and there was no guessing what his thought might be at work upon behind that drowsy glance"

(395). The idyll continues when they climb out of the river together:

> We dried off before the fire, without haste. To need no clothes is better than purple and fine linen. Then he tossed the flap-jacks and I served the trout, and after this we lay on our backs upon the buffalo hide to smoke and watch the Tetons grow more solemn, as the large stars opened out over the sky.
> "I don't care if I never go home," said I.
> The Virginian nodded. "It gives all the peace o' being asleep with all the pleasure o' feeling the widest kind of awake," said he. "Yu' might say the whole year's strength flows hearty in every waggle of your thumb." (397)

Since the partners are still naked at this point, it would be difficult to believe that their thumbs are the only appendages waggling with a "whole year's strength" flowing through them. (A year, remember, has passed since they last saw each other.) Their contentment includes a degree of tolerance for erotic closeness in this isolated spot, elevating it with superlatives about perception: super-deep sleep, the widest kind of wakefulness, and extra-hearty strength. Now, finally, the Virginian feels comfortable enough to talk about what has been on his mind.

He speaks about a ruffian cowboy named Hank, who has married an Austrian immigrant named Willomene, a devout Catholic whose English isn't so good. Her worship of her crucifix, and her guileless kindnesses to the Virginian and other bachelor cowboys in their camp, cause Hank to grow jealous and abusive. The narrator wonders why Hank wanted to marry Willomene in the first place, to which the Virginian replies,

> "Why any man would," he answered. "I wanted her myself, till I found out she was good."
> I looked at this son of the wilderness, standing thoughtful and splendid by the fire, and unconscious of his own religion that had unexpectedly shone forth in these last words. But I said nothing; for words too intimate, especially words of esteem, put him invariably to silence. (399)

Whether a woman is "good" in nineteenth-century literature usually means determining not only if she is a virgin, but also if she is chaste, modest, passive, and devout.[7] The Virginian's nonchalant confession implies that his lust for a bad woman, a perfectly respectable feeling in the cowboy code, ends in the presence of feminine goodness, which drives his desire underground. The narrator calls the Virginian's words a "religion that had unexpectedly shone forth," and he worships the unselfconscious pagan for having admitted what no East Coast gentleman ever would. He suppresses the language of praise he wishes he could lavish upon him; "But I said nothing," knowing that masculine indifference, not feminine esteem, is the path to closer intimacy.[8]

In silent adoration, the narrator listens while the Virginian continues to speak his religious principles during this extraordinary scene. He tells the narrator more about Willomene and Hank. It is a disturbing story about a soon-to-be fatal mix of a "good" woman pushed to her limits by her abusive husband. Before he begins telling this tale, the Virginian announces its moral first: "not any such thing as a fam'ly for me, yet. Never, it may be. Not till I can't help it. And *that* woman has not come along so far" (398, emphasis in orginal).[9]

To this news the narrator responds with rapture. What thrills the narrator so much is that the Virginian vows never to marry, never to have a family. His devotion to bachelorhood strikes the narrator as the very essence of free-spirited manhood in the West. This "son of the wilderness" who fries fish in the nude and who discusses deep thoughts without knowing much about books is a priest espousing a religion of Pan. He eschews Christianity, scoffs at monogamy, and indulges in lusts that are prohibited in East Coast society.[10] But most important of all, he confides in the narrator, bringing them closer than just friends.

Wister himself waited to marry until he was 38 years old, in 1898. Like his cowboy character, he settled down after taking his wife on a month-long horseback honeymoon, and after his children were born he journeyed West far less frequently than he did as a bachelor. Less is known about his friendships with men, formed and lost in the years before he was married. Starting in 1885, on the advice of a physician treating him for "nervousness," Wister, then 25 years old, boarded a train in New York, and went to Big Horn Basin in Wyoming. The experience transformed him, not only curing him of his nervousness, but also inspiring him to write fiction instead of practice law. Every year thereafter he returned, keeping copious journals and traveling with his special friend, George West, who took him on frequent and lengthy hunting trips. George West was a young man Wister described in a letter to his mother as "24 and much too good-looking. He is much better looking than any of us" (Seelye, xvi). Of one of their hunting trips, Wister writes, "these Wind River days with George West had an enchantment that no doubt can never be wrought again" (*Journals* 20). As their friendship developed, Wister funded West's attempt to build a ranch, and until West's requests for money became too frequent, their correspondence was peppered with fond and loving phrases.[11] After an unrecorded altercation, Wister stopped writing to West.

In his journals as well as his Western short stories, Wister in his bachelor years was drawn to men who in one way or another rejected marriage or traditional courtship rituals. He wrote for example on July 17, 1893, about a young stagecoach driver whom he found attractive, doubly so when their talk turns to the subject of failed connections with women:

> I sat beside the driver, whose name was Hunter, and he certainly was a jewel. He was handsome, and with that fascination that so many of his kind have. He mentioned he had never had any luck with women, and of course we exchange views and notes upon this inexhaustible subject. (174)

The good-looking Westerner is just a typical "jewel" to Wister until Hunter mentions that he has no "luck with women, whereupon" Wister becomes fascinated, and he is moved to confess his own lack of success with women. The subtext to this conversation is intimacy; Wister feels closer to a handsome man who has no luck with women because he, too, is unattached.

In another journal entry written in Texas in 1885, he overhears Tom King, one of the living prototypes for the fictional cowboy in *The Virginian*, claim that "cowboys never live long enough to get old." Thinking about it later, Wister remarks, "They're a queer episode in the history of this country. Purely nomadic, and leaving no posterity, for they don't marry. I'm told they're without any moral sense whatever" (*Journals* 39). Their temporary status in the history of the United States intrigues him. He relishes their bachelor freedoms and their lack of moral sense. Perhaps like James Fenimore Cooper, Wister felt that bachelor-frontiersmen need novelists like him to

Illustration 8 Owen Wister based his famous character from *The Virginian*, in part, on his long-time friend and wilderness guide, George West, the seated figure on the left. Wister is standing and pouring a drink. Detail from "Wister's Hunting Party in Camp at Jackson Hole, Wyoming, 1887." American Heritage Center, Owen Wister Collection, accession number 290.

document their accomplishments, since they leave behind no posterity.[12] If so, Wister appointed himself the task for at least two decades, producing many stories of the West, none of them so successful nor so finely wrought as *The Virginian*, the book that would define his career as a writer forever after. His literary project, then, is tied to elevating a figure "without any moral sense whatever" to the status of hero, mythologizing him as an icon of unrestrained masculinity and an ideal for others to live up to.

In his Western stories, Wister prefers the plainspoken immorality of cowboys to the false morality of airless East Coast society.[13] Moreover, he associates cowboy immorality in the West with the best of American national characteristics. In *The Virginian*, the narrator studies the handsome faces of "cow-boys at their play" in a saloon. "Here were lusty horsemen," he crows, "Youth untamed sat here." Comparing the Western saloon with bars in New York, the narrator prefers the saloon. "More of death it undoubtedly saw, but less of vice, than did its New York equivalents. And death is a thing much cleaner than vice" (25). Wrinkling his nose at the dirtiness of vice in New York bars, the narrator almost breaks into a patriotic song when he sees the cleaner, if not more violent, immoralities of "lusty horsemen . . . cow-boys at their play." "Daring, laughter, endurance,—these were what I saw upon the countenances of the cow-boys . . . something about them, and the idea of them, smote my American heart, and I have never forgotten it . . . In their flesh our natural passions ran tumultuous" (25).

Wister's elevated diction in the phrase "natural passions ran tumultuous" uses a kind of stylistic quiver that ripples throughout *The Virginian* whenever the narrator waxes rhapsodic about his friend's handsomeness and tiger-like muscles. The narrator's love affair with the black-haired horseman has national dimensions as well as artistic ones; the new nation, with its new, and newly expanding frontier, produced a new type of man, bred in the wilds of North America, elevated above the sickly urbanites of late-nineteenth-century capitalism. Cowboys stand second to nobody; they practice rowdy vices without guilt. When Wister swells with patriotic pride upon glimpsing this unsullied manhood of cowboys in an immoral context, he projects upon the nation an idealization of manhood that resists marriage, withholds desire for "good" women, and promotes coded homoerotic intimacies with same-sex partners in the wilderness.

Illustration 9 Charles M. Russell contrasts illustrated violence with words of affection in this illustration of cowboy supremacy over East Coast dandyism. "Dance! You Short Horn Dance!" ink and transparent watercolor over graphite underdrawing on paper, 1907. By Charles M. Russell. Amon Carter Museum accession number 1961.310.

After several hundred pages of conflict, resistance, coyness, humiliation, and bravery, Molly Stark Wood, the schoolmarm, finally marries the Virginian, surrendering her feisty adherence to spinsterhood just as the Virginian surrenders his. The difference is that the Virginian has been on at least one honeymoon before, when he stood naked before the silent narrator and spouted Pan's philosophies. The two honeymoons mirror each other, but the second is decidedly less erotic.

The Virginian takes Molly to an island in a mountain stream on the eastern slopes of the Tetons, but this island is not as far from the beaten path as the island where he took the narrator. Theirs was an island far deeper in the wilderness, in a territory more rugged and remote. Instead of "Truth parading around undressed," modesty is the rule on the bride and groom's island, with separate tents for dressing, and separate sides of the island for bathing. Instead of partners celebrating nudity, bachelorhood, and waggling thumbs in the great outdoors, the Virginian won't let Molly see him naked at all, nor will he allow her to see him unshaven or without his "soft silk neckerchief knotted with care" (383). The Virginian becomes soft for his wife; he relinquishes hardness, resolve, thirst, and his adherence to an impulse-driven body. Not only modesty but also the diminished grandeur of language and symbol suggest the twilight of manhood for this marriage, rather than the robust youth and playfully bohemian excesses of the males-only version. Instead of mountain stags or tigers using "the elemental talk of sex," the diminutive mink carries the homoerotic parable, burying it in the past and in the wilderness.

"If this book be anything more than an American story," writes Wister in the Preface of the 1911 edition of his book, "it is an expression of American faith" (li). Some of the doctrines of this faith run against the grain of civilized society, and Wister's novel illustrates how these rebellious ideologies are driven underground once the wilderness disappears. The mink scampers off into the woods, and the frontier closes, erasing the homoerotic bonds and the previous vows not to marry. This famous nonjoiner finally joins the institution he so soundly rejected.

Before Wister's revision of the cowboy's story, Westerns usually ended with the hero riding off into the sunset, when their work was done, perhaps into sequels; or he died in some spectacular and melodramatic way, leaving behind just a partner and sometimes his horse. Literally hundreds of dime novel Westerns and popular magazine tales about frontiersmen followed Cooper's example, and avoided male–female romance-driven plots altogether. This solution was possible, apparently, as long as there was unconquered territory in the fabled West to occupy. In texts with titles such as *Young Mountaineer; Daring Davy, the Young Bear Killer; Buffalo Bill's Queer Find;* and *Buck Taylor*, the popular presses churned out adventure stories where male characters undergo all kinds of dangerous challenges and life-threatening dilemmas with legendary bravado, but when it comes to feminine or domestic influences, the heroes of these popular novels rely on cowardice alone.

Wister's romance, as I have said, was extremely popular, and its appeal helped to shift the Western paradigm. Most Westerns of the twentieth century engage the cowboy–schoolmarm romance motif that Wister introduced. Several historians of sexuality have noted a simultaneous rise in intolerance for certain behaviors associated with same-sex erotic practices. Prior to the invention of the "homosexual" as an illness, U.S. culture tolerated a great deal of same-sex erotic touching, kissing, bed-sharing, and bathing, whether in East Coast cities or in Western prairies.[14] The literature produced during this time reflects a tacit cultural approval of such practices. Portrait photography of couples and groups from this period encourages same-sex intimate touching while enforcing opposite sex isolation.[15] *The Virginian* includes language documenting this tradition, and attributing to it emotional qualities bespeaking intimacy. Still, Wister forecloses the possibility of lifelong male partnerships by having the Virginian hang up his spurs and marry Molly Wood in the end.

"Nothing," wrote Henry James, "should have induced me to unite [the Virginian] to the little Vermont person, or to dedicate him in fact to achieved parentage, prosperity, maturity.... I thirst for his blood. I wouldn't have let him live & be happy: I should have made him perish in his flower & in some splendid somber way."[16] James was probably not raised on dime novels, but his plot revision for Wister's novel reveals he has inculcated the expectation that Western heroes cannot marry nor produce a family; their fate is to die as they lived, "in some splendid somber way," like Leatherstocking, in Cooper's *The Prairie*, who dies in a blaze of sunset and glory.

One frequent marker of the bonds between partners is the handsomeness of one and the effect of those good looks on the other. The narrator of *The Virginian* often remarks upon the handsome face and tiger-like body of his partner, and his identification with a wife's pleasure when he catches a smoldering expression is a clearly erotic effect. Similarly, when Bareback Buck rides up to a wagon train in *Bareback Buck, Centaur of the Plains*, a Beadle and Adams dime novel by Philip Warne, the young narrator is stunned by his first impression: "With straight, black hair and a swarthy complexion, he looked not unlike a half-breed Indian; and his coal-black eyes had an intensity of gaze that had set to tingling the nerves of men who had passed for fairly plucky."[17] Forever after, this image motivates the young Argonaut to be Buck's partner. The "tingling of nerves" is a telling response to dashing Buck's good looks, and they foretell a loving future for the two robust roughriders. After a book's worth of thrilling danger, the two decide to stick together, riding off into the sunset, but not into the arms of a woman. Both have failed to win the heart of feisty and fickle Rose, but in the process they have become inseparable buddies. The Centaur of the Plains proclaims the narrator is his "pard, and a staunch pard he makes, too" (29). The narrator is thrilled to have earned this title.

Good looks in cowboy culture often mean the slouchy, relaxed, "natural" looks like the image of Walt Whitman that appears in the frontispiece to the 1855 edition of *Leaves of Grass*, or the Virginian's man-of-ease. Handsomeness in Mexicans, Mestizo, and Indian tribesmen is also an important feature of literary heroes of the popular press. Very often in the racist language of the day, writers associated dark-skinned figures such as Mestizos with animalistic sexuality. Here, the swarthy Joaquín Murieta (1868) is lavished with superlatives, none of which modify his intellect:

> His . . . countenance is pronounced to have been, at that time, exceedingly handsome and attractive. His large black eyes, kindling with the enthusiasm of his earnest nature, his firm and well-formed mouth, his well-shaped head from which the long, glossy, black hair hung down over his shoulders, his silvery voice full of generous utterance, and the frank and cordial bearing which distinguished him made him beloved by all with whom he came in contact.[18] (8–9)

Choose any of the adjectives and you will find seductive appeal. His body too is "gracefully built, and active as a young tiger." Ridge suggests through overwrought metaphors that Murieta imposes his good looks as a way to command and lead; they are a form of power that make him "beloved by all with whom he came in contact."

Herman Melville in his posthumously published *Billy Budd, Sailor*, written just a decade before *The Virginian*, has theorized the effect of handsomeness on all-male communities.[19] Although working in the genre of sea tales, his discussion of how handsomeness organizes all-male communities into quasi-democracies applies to Westerns as well.

Like Hercules among mortals, Billy Budd is handsome sailor, a natural leader of groups of less good-looking men. Melville describes how the uglier mates hand over authority in exchange for homosocial privileges. Seemingly entitled by his beauty, the handsome sailor smoothes over petty troubles in the all-male worlds of ships and docks, spreading goodwill and *bonne homme* spirit. Melville describes as an example, a good-looking sailor

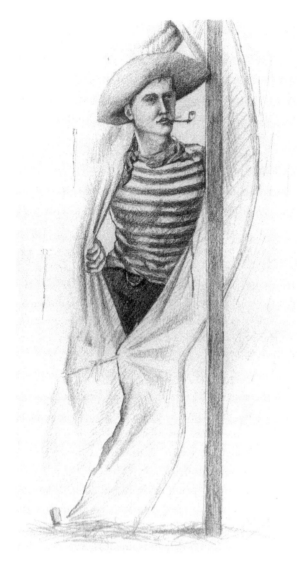

Illustration 10 Frederic Remington called this "Hello, Old Boy," one of his earliest drawings. As the young cowboy parts the flaps of the artist's tent, his Venus de Milo pose suggests erotic undertones as he seeks the permission of the artist and the viewer to proceed. "Hello, Old Boy," graphite on paper. By Frederic Remington. The Frederic Remington Art Museum.

from Africa he once spotted on the Liverpool docks: "a symmetric figure much above the average height." With big gold hoops in his ears and a brawny chest exposed, his face "beamed with barbaric good humor," and "he rollicked along, the center of a company of his shipmates." So good-looking is this man that passersby stop and stare. "At each spontaneous tribute rendered by wayfarers to this black pagod of a fellow," the group surrounding their superior mate basks in the pride of worshippers whose faith in their deity has been confirmed.[20] The effect of handsomeness upon all-male groups is to inspire devotion, worship, and greater faith in the larger enterprise instead of isolating self-interest. But in Billy Budd's case, being handsome also subverts established power balances, robbing others of authority, and perhaps causing insurrection, rivalry, or mutinous rage. As Melville puts it, "comeliness and power [are] always attractive in masculine conjunction," and his last story, left unfinished at his death in 1891, explored both the erotic and the fatal aspects of males-only desires. Wister too explored the effect of a handsome cowboy on lesser men, linking it to a national pride.

An exact contemporary of Owen Wister, Andy Adams in *A Texas Matchmaker* takes up these feudal themes in an attempt to stitch together the cowboy novel of adventure with the romance novel. Whereas Wister's cowboy novel shifts the paradigm, Adams's book upholds an earlier pattern, where the frontiersman rejects marriage to women. Uncle Lance Lovelace is the appealing leader of a band of white cowboys on his ranch in South Texas, organizing their allegiance like satellites revolving around a star. According to Tom Quirk, the youthful narrator, Lovelace is "a man of simple tastes, true as tested steel in his friendships" (3).

As a self-designated matchmaker, Lovelace wants his ranch hands to meet and marry white women so he can populate his ranch with white babies. He also arranges marriage for the *vaqueros* on his ranch, acting in this capacity as a *padrón*, a linguistic hybrid of *padre* and *patrón*. His own failures as a husband do not bode well for his plan: his first wife died in childbirth, far from medical help, and two subsequent marriages, "unhappy alliances" with slatternly women, are dissolved almost without mention (3–4). Still, Lovelace cites his success with breeding horses and Mexican vaqueros as evidence of his skill as a matchmakers. To a man, the whites fail to make matches with anyone except Uncle Lance, to whom they devote themselves like wives of a harem, but Mexicans are inordinately successful breeders. "Honest, boys," complains Lovelace to his white ranch hands, "I'm getting disgusted with the white element of [my ranch]. We raise most everything here but white babies I reckon the Caucasian is played out" (127).

A Texas Matchmaker was not nearly as successful as Adams's first novel, *The Log of a Cowboy*, published just a year earlier, perhaps because Adams refused to let his privileged cowboys marry and have children. Quirk's quirk is that his allegiance to Uncle Lance and his ranching enterprise conflicts with his half-hearted attempts to find a girl and settle down. The same goes for the others in Lovelace's outfit. As one of the more experienced cowboys says, "I generally keep a wire fence between them [women] and myself if they show any symptoms of being on the marry" (170). The homosocial order in *A Texas Matchmaker* makes clear that marriage is an obstacle that the white cowboys cannot overcome. "[T]here's something about cattle life which I can't explain," laments Lovelace at the end of *A Texas Matchmaker*. "It seems to disqualify a man for ever making a good citizen afterward. He roams and runs around, wasting his youth, and gets so foxy he never marries" (353). The trouble with wives in Westerns, at least until Wister's *The Virginian* came along, is that they come with a doctrine that annihilates the identity of a free spirited cowboy. But as Wister showed, the partnership with a same-sex friend, when it resembles a marriage, provides safety, consolation, and perhaps erotic satisfaction either prior to marriage or alongside it.[21]

Like many of the dime novel Westerns, *Live Boys; or, Charley and Nasho in Texas* features several opportunities for two 14 year olds—one a white cowboy, the other a Mexican/Kickapoo vaquero—to practice their intimate and erotic friendship.[22] Lost in a blizzard, for example, Charley falls from his horse, unconscious and near death from freezing. He wakes up two hours later, undressed and wrapped in a blanket with Nasho, who explains, "You 'most froze, . . . Carley [*sic*]. You was lying on ground and me couldn't wake you up. Me hurry and make fire and heat pot of water. Den me stretch tent and take off your clothes and dip blanket in hot water, and wrap you up in him" (301). With Charley now revived, Nasho soon succumbs to the effects of hypothermia. Charley finishes building the sweatlodge that Nasho started, stretching the animal skins over the tent while heating river stones in a fire. "Then I woke Nasho up and at last got him to understand that he must undress and get in. I helped him, for he was more than half asleep" The sweat-lodge restores Nasho to health, and after rolling him in the snow, Charley "rubbed him dry, covered him up well with blankets, gave him some hot tea" (302).

Live Boys is full of these kinds of intimate, half-dressed encounters under animal hides in wilderness contexts. Each contributes to the theme of close bonds between the boys. Nasho is of particular interest to Charley because he is "strange and wild" (19)—a nonwhite boy of the wilderness who teaches him the survival skills of the Kickapoo. Nasho is an illiterate savage from the school of Rousseau, who can slit a grizzly's throat or scalp an outlaw without showing any emotion or remorse. "He's a curious fellow," Charley concludes about his silent, loyal buddy. "He don't ever get excited like most boys" (66). As a playmate for a 14-year-old white orphan, Nasho is an ideal adventure partner who never says no, whether the adventure means hunting a panther or sharing a bunk with Charley every night. The erotic quality of their friendship is evident in actions, not words; their closeness is instinctive but silent: "Indians don't say much," Charley explains, "especially the young ones" (67). But in more intimate moments, immediately following a crisis or a near-escape from death, Nasho does occasionally release a signal of his deeper feelings. "Me mighty glad to see you," Nasho tells Charley upon finding him alive after a 20-mile bareback ride on a renegade horse. Charley replies he is mighty glad to see Nasho too. "There ain't many American boys that would have followed me up as he did. Nasho'll do to trust every time if he likes anybody" (99).

Writing for the *Atlantic* in 1907, Charles M. Harvey waxed nostalgic for his favorite form of boyhood escapist literature: "The aim of the original dime novel was to give, in cheap and wholesome form, a picture of American wild life" (42). Harvey's insistence upon wholesomeness is rather at odds with the bloody tortures, murders, kidnappings, and shoot-'em-ups that drench every page of these "blood and thunder" tales, told with their unabashedly purple prose, melodrama, and formulaic repetition. More accurate is Harvey's assertion that dime novel Westerns gave pictures of "American wild life" in sensational, thrilling ways. To be sure, they served important moral and cultural purposes: to teach "[m]anliness ... among readers. ... not by homilies, but by example" (43).

Examples of American life in the wilderness include Daredeath Dick, King of the Cowboys, slaying savages by the dozen (but loving the exception—his sexy Indian guide—with remarkable intensity); the renegade Girty, who could bulldog the orneriest critter alive by biting its lip and wrestling it to the dust, and whose only nonviolent intimacy comes with his bunk buddy; Three-Fingered Jack, who laughed while torturing and murdering lawmen foolish enough to follow his outlaw's trail; the Virginian, who lynches his ex-best-friend Steve while proposing honeymoons and pagan practices with the narrator; Joaquín Murieta, the Celebrated California Bandit; the fearless Geronimo, Chief of the Apaches. All these characters teach "manliness," American style, by testing their metal against adversaries in the Western wilderness, but knowing too when to strike homoerotic unions in the name of survival. Violence, cunning, and ruthlessness are prime qualities for manliness, but coinciding with these is affection for certain cherished same-sex partners.

The writers discussed so far in this chapter, unlike Cooper in the previous, each experienced the "wild" West first hand.[23] Wister traveled every summer to Wyoming, keeping copious journals while getting away from New York City and the cloying wiles of urban East Coast sophisticates. He enjoyed traveling on horseback in clear, healthful, masculine regions with his close friend George West. Andy Adams was a scrappy runaway teenager in 1874, rounding up cattle in the years before barbed wire, and for a time surviving as a horse dealer in Caldwell, Kansas before turning to writing. Little is known of Philip Warne, except for the dozen or so novels he produced for Beadle and Adams. These stories of the Mississippi River and adjacent states on the West show that he was familiar with the region about which he wrote.[24] Charles Siringo called himself "an old stove-up cowpuncher" at age 30, when he stopped cowboying and started to build his career as a writer of *A Texas Cowboy*.[25]

Frederic Loring also went out West early in 1871 in order to experience it first hand and to write about it. The 22 year old had just graduated from Harvard, about a decade before Owen Wister would graduate from the same institution.[26] Before leaving the East Coast, Loring was working at the Boston *Saturday Evening Gazette*, and his play had enjoyed a popular run in a Boston theater during his senior year. His novel, *Two College Friends*, was about to be published by his uncle's press. His stories and poems had already appeared in the *Atlantic Monthly* in Boston, and the *Independent*, the *World*, and *Appleton's Journal* in New York. On the basis of these promising accomplishments, Loring was hired by *Appleton's Journal* to accompany an expedition to survey the southeast corner of Nevada, the upper waters of the Colorado River, and the Arizona Territory. His obituary in the *New York Times*, written just nine months after he left, reports that "a band of 50 Apache Indians" attacked his stagecoach, about ten miles outside of Wickenburg, Arizona, in early November, 1871.[27] The driver and five passengers were killed. "Their personal effects were not disturbed."

Loring was probably on his way back to San Francisco, having spent eight months with the expedition, crossing Death Valley at least once and traversing the canyons around it. In his last published article, "Into the Valley of Death," he joked that his beard was so thick he could be mistaken for a "forty-niner in the world, but a seventy-oner in California."

The stagecoach attack was not the first Indian hostility Loring had encountered. Just two months earlier, he hastily scribbled a note in pencil to his editors at *Appleton's Journal*:

> We are laid up crippled and helpless in this desert. Lieutenant Wheeler is taking these letters to a mail-station, which we hope, after he brings us relief, to reach in three days. I have had a fortnight of horrors—this morning an Indian fight capped the climax. At the present date, however, I am well and cheerful. As soon as I can copy them I will send extracts from my journal. This may be the last, however, that you will hear from me if we don't get out or get reënforcements [*sic*] soon.

His letter blames a Shoshone Indian chief, Cowitch, for the attack that left him "bootless, coatless, everything but lifeless." The language he uses to describe his situation swings between extremes. He is "crippled and helpless" in one sentence, and "I am well and cheerful" in another. He predicts his own death if reinforcements don't come soon, but he promises writeups and discusses his payment. After characterizing the recent Indian attack, facetiously, as "kind treatment," Loring blames the savage wilderness around him for scrambling his logic: "My letter is incoherent, but who could help getting mixed up in such a country as this? The ghastly absurdity of my recent experiences makes me laugh in spite of my being somewhat scared at what I fear is still to come." His fearful laughter at the "ghastly absurdity" of his situation is a far cry from the droll dandyisms and crudely racist humor in his article about Cowitch, the Shoshone chief, whom Loring blames for the attack.

Loring's account of his interview with Cowitch, published just two weeks before the attack, deserves inspection because it reveals how masculine discourse in the West balanced upon a razor's edge between intimacy and violence. In all of his articles, Loring affects the tone of a sophisticated wit observing what is vile and low, inviting his audiences back East to enjoy his arch observations and coy innuendoes rely upon racist stereotypes of the most pernicious kind. "[T]he proper method of talking to an Indian," he writes, "is to say 'heap' as often as possible [and] omit all prepositions and conjunctions." Loring's interview hopes to glean "some ethnological information" from Cowitch, but the Shoshone chief controls the conversation from the start.

> Then Cowitch asked me if I had a squaw.
>
> I told him not at present, but there was no saying what might happen, to which he assented, with the luminous observation, "Yes, heap happen," which was certainly truthful, if not profound.
>
> Then, as a return question, I asked him if those were his squaws, and he acknowledge them. I asked him still further if he could *sabe* Mormon.
>
> He could not, and I explained as follows: "Mormon—tribe—over there—Salt Lake—big chief heap squaws—ten—twenty—sixty—heap squaws."
>
> What do you suppose was this sagacious chieftain's response? I glow with delight as I write it.
>
> "No fun—heap squaws—no fun."[28]

Loring glows with delight when he reports the "sagacious chieftain's" confession, just as the narrator glowed with pleasure when the Virginian vowed never to marry. Two men who bond over confessions of wifelessness, or chuckle over the problem of too many wives, participate in a code that separates them from their adherence to domesticity, creating momentary harmony between them based upon a misogynist conspiracy. That a prissy, Harvard-educated bachelor and a Shoshone chief in war paint can see eye to eye on the subject of wives testifies to the power of homosocial privilege. Their alliance is short lived, and Loring concludes his piece with contemptuous words for those who "prate about the wrongs of the noble savage, who is, generally speaking, a filthy and degraded brute" (183).

Perhaps Loring got the end he deserved. Having been terrorized at least once already by Indians from Cowitch's band, he was killed by Apaches. However, poetic justice is a literary conceit, not a way to explain a murder, no matter how egregious the offender's language. Loring was killed along with five others. What he left behind is a handful of articles that deride Indians, Mormons, and Chinese.

So too might have William W. Chamberlain wished to murder his former Harvard classmate, after Loring dedicated his novel, *Two College Friends*, to him. In fact, Loring predicted Chamberlain's "indignation" at such a dedication. The preface takes the form of a personal letter written from Loring to Chamberlain that he purports to be writing in San Francisco:

> Indignation at my dedicating this book to you will be useless since I am at present three thousand miles out of your reach. Moreover, this dedication is not intended as a public monument to our friendship;—I know too much for that. If that were the case, we should manage to quarrel even at this distance, I am quite confident, before the proof-sheets had left the press. But I can dedicate it to you alone of all my college friends, because you and I were brought so especially into the atmosphere of the man who inspired me to undertake it. (3)

Why would Chamberlain be indignant at such a laudatory preface? Loring predicts a quarrel over whether the dedication is "a public monument to our friendship," but he stands by his dedication—"to you alone of all my college friends"—because Chamberlain enjoyed with Loring the special support of "the man who inspired me" to write *Two College Friends*. This man was probably Elbridge J. Cutler, a poet and a professor of modern languages at Harvard, who died a year before Loring's book came out.

There is no record of Chamberlain's response, nor even evidence that he read his former Harvard classmate's book. No reviews were published, and even Loring's Harvard class notes ignore the title of this book and dismiss it with a phrase.[29] It was never reprinted. Its lack of attention perhaps resides in its lack of quality; the book is maudlin, despotic, and dimly plotted. Still, its intensely homoerotic language, and its dated depiction of muscular, robust, patriotic friendship deserves attention here because it is autobiographical.

Two College Friends presents Ned and Tom at Harvard College, undergraduate gadflies of the privileged classes gallivanting beneath the elms in the Yard, until President Lincoln declares war, at which point they join the Union army and fight to defend the nation's unity. Ned is killed in a decisive battle at the end, and Tom survives, having been saved by the valorous Ned. In an afterword, Tom names his first son after Ned. The preface suggests that the fictional Ned is Loring, the fictional Tom is Chamberlain, and the fictional professor is meant to be Cutler.

In the book's climactic scene, Ned saves Tom's life by helping him escape from a group of Confederate soldiers. On a point of honor, Ned must return to custody, having promised Stonewall Jackson himself he would do so. While Ned says goodbye to his companion, probably for the last time, Tom is unconscious with a fever. Tom's inability to answer—to quarrel, to be indignant—perhaps allows Ned to express his deepest feelings about him:

> O my darling, my darling, my darling! Please hear me. The only one I have ever loved at all, the only one who has ever loved me. . . . O Tom, my darling! don't forget it. If you know how I love you, how I have loved you in all my jealous, morbid moods, in all my exacting selfishness,—O Tom! my darling, my darling! Can't you say one word, one little word before we part. (129)

Ned is the more demonstrative of the pair, while Tom is far better looking. They meet for the first time in their professor's study, and share a glass of Madiera. "The moment I saw Tom, I felt drawn towards him," Ned remarks privately. Tom is equally enthralled with Ned—he is "radiant with enjoyment, with the firelight tinting his lovely face" (26–28)—and they soon become roommates. There are tender moments, like when Tom admires an Etruscan locket of Ned's, who has Tom's initials cut on it to give to him (92); and there are jealous tiffs, like the one that erupts over a photograph, when

Ned accuses Tom of letting a classmate replace him as Tom's best chum. When Ned insists that Tom must "choose between us," Tom replies, "I don't care for any fellow as I do for you" (32). The professor comments that their affair is like the meeting of "sunbeam and volcano."

Their intimate declarations of love and petulant quarrels continue, whether they pair under the elms in Harvard Hard or on the Virginia battlefields. Ned earns rank as a lieutenant, while Tom is his captain. Together they lead with muscular bravado a troop of Union soldiers into battles with "that restless creature, Stonewall Jackson." During one battle, Ned and Tom aren't on speaking terms. When Tom saves Ned's life by killing the soldier about to shoot him, Ned says thank you. Tom declares triumphantly, " 'you spoke first.' I saw that I had, and I was dreadfully provoked" (81–82). Their boyish and roughhouse affection balances tender moments, as when Ned records in his journal, "I wonder if I shall ever care for any woman as much as I do for Tom" (47); or later, Ned writes, "When this war is over, I suppose Tom will marry and forget me. I shall never go near his wife—I shall hate her" (84). So passionate is their friendship that an enemy soldier recognizes its similarity to the love between men and women: "You care for him about as you would for a gal, don't you?" the Rebel soldier says after witnessing Ned taking care of the unconscious Tom. Ned's affirmation is implied when the soldier acknowledges, "Well, he's pootier than any gal I ever see anywhar" (120). Based on his admiration for these hero-lovers, the "Virginia barbarian" helps them escape. Here again homoerotic privilege unites enemies.

Ned returns to captivity, as I have said, because he promised Stonewall Jackson he would. His loyalty to honor supercedes his passionate desire to stay beside his wounded friend. During his goodbye soliloquy over Tom's unconscious body, Ned speaks of a picture they had quarreled about back at Harvard. "I have it now, Tom; it will be with me when they bury me." This picture is of Tom dressed as a "dear little peasant girl" (36) in theatrical makeup and costume, playing the role of "Marton, the Pride of the Market." The Professor's remarks about this photograph are revealing: "What a mistake nature made about your sex, Tom."

Ned does die with Tom's picture tucked near to his heart, shot just once at the very moment the bugle announces that reinforcements have arrived. "He stood there strong, like a man; and then there was one report, and he fell dead,—dead in the dust of the Virginia soil" (153). In an afterword, Loring writes how Ned's dead body has been haunting him

> Even in the wild regions of Nevada and the undulating lawns and woody slopes of California. In the snow-clad forests of the Sierra Nevada, and even in the tropical glory of sky and air in Arizona, and the noise and bustle of camp, with heavenly peace and loveliness above, and murderous savages, thirsting for our blood lying in deadly ambush all around, I still have seen the picture. (154)

His point seems to be that the picture of Ned's death (who himself holds a picture of Tom impersonating a woman), superimposed upon the Western landscapes, suggests a relationship between martyrdom in the name of honor on the Civil War battlefield and the conquest of the American West. "This wonderful country, that is still in its infancy, that is still nursing men of every nation to form a new nation . . . justifies not merely enthusiasm but any loss of human life which may aid in its preservation" (160–161). With this patriotic justification for murder and sacrifice in the name of U.S. imperialism, Loring glorifies Ned's death as a sacrifice that a man must make for a "new nation," and designates Tom, as the surviving partner, with the duty to populate the "new country" through conventional means, memorializing his friend by naming his son Ned.

In this ending, Loring attempts what Wister achieves in *The Virginian*, the graceful combination of antimarriage, antifeminine adventure tales with a simultaneous domestic plot that culminates in a marriage. Unlike Wister, Loring martyrs his hero in a blaze of glory, upholding the earlier tradition established by Cooper, where the frontier hero never marries, but moves perpetually westward into a setting sun. All three writers were attempting to write tales that captured their experiences as young men in frontier situations: Cooper in northern New York State in the early 1800s, Loring in the Nevada and Arizona Territories in the 1870s, and Wister in the Wyoming Territory and Texas in the 1880s and 1890s. All three were men of elite status in Anglo-American culture, well-educated and urbane, who saw themselves as interpreters of actual Western experience.

Marriage is the familiar metaphor they used in order to measure the quality of male-male friendships in the West. Ridiculing marriage is a dominant motif in *The Virginian*, and even after the cowboy is married his observation of the mink during his honeymoon reveals some regret in abandoning his status as a bachelor-cowboy. Loring ridicules the polygamy practiced by Shoshone tribal elders and Mormons, while coyly appreciating a handsome Indian translator. In his *Two College Friends*, Ned and Tom practice schoolboy crushes that when carried out onto a Civil War battlefield turn into tragedy. Whether making fun of marriage, or using it to explain how serious the partnerships can be between national heroes, the stories favored by readers in the United States after the Civil War celebrated male–male partnerships over female–male unions whenever the scenery shifted to the mythical Western wilderness.

CHAPTER THREE

AMERICAN SATYRIASIS IN WHITMAN, HARRIS, AND HARTLAND

I call this chapter American satyriasis because each of the three writers considered here associate a literary version of satyriasis, also known as Don Juanism, or more recently, sex addiction, with American manhood and nation building in the West. This motif of perpetual erotic arousal is best articulated in Whitman's poetry and prose about "camaraderie" in the West. Frank Harris also connects perpetual sexual indulgences with the heights of literary ecstasy and freedoms of young men in Kansas in the 1870s. Claude Hartland's autobiography, *The Story of a Life*, characterizes satyriasis as an "animal spirit" that overcomes his reason and compels him to have multiple male sex partners in and around St. Louis during the 1890s. Hartland's sexual confession defines, if not a nation, at least a community of temporary lovers, and the doctors who would cure them, in the city known as the Gateway to the West. Whitman, Harris, and Hartland, in other words, developed a poetics of homoeroticism in the last quarter of the nineteenth century, and associated it with the American West.

In an interview published in *The St. Louse Post-Dispatch* on October 17, 1879, Walt Whitman said, "My idea of one great feature of future American poetry is the expression of comradeship. That is a main point with me."[1] This "comradeship"—which Whitman defined as "manly attachment"—is best expressed in the "superb masculinity of the West," where he believed the "dominion-heart of America" would come to reside.

Illustration 11 In history and in literature the Stag Dance was a common passtime among cow hands whether out on the trail or in the bunk house. Detail from "Dancing, seemingly not hampered by lack of women," Gelatin dry plate negative, 1901–1915, by Erwin E. Smith. Amon Carter Museum accession number LC-S6-058.

The West was so important to America in the post–Civil War period, according to Whitman, that the U.S. Capitol itself would one day "migrate a thousand or two miles" inland.

Whitman wonders in a speech called "The Prairies" that appeared in *The St. Louis Dispatch* in 1881 if "the people of this continental inland West know how much of first-class *art* they have in these prairies . . ." (853). In speaking of "*art*," he means not only the beautiful landscape, but also the Americans living in and imbibing this extraordinary beauty. The inland states and territories "are equally and integrally and indissolubly

Illustration 12 Whitman celebrates "manly attachment" by cataloging its best qualities: youth, robust Western masculinity, animal appetites, and large-bodied, healthy men who refuse all doctrines except democracy. "Pioneer Mining in California," by Andre Castaigne. *The Century*, May 1891.

this Nation, the *sine qua non* of the human, political and commercial New World . . . the home of what I would call America's distinctive ideas and distinctive realities" (asterisks in the original, 854).

Whitman's prediction about the Capitol never came true, but his prediction of the importance of Western masculinity to American aesthetic possibilities did. (It is perhaps not surprising that Whitman's poems themselves attempt to scale this gargantuan literary achievement.) He describes men of the West in superlatives organized around robust physicality: a "solid personality, with blood and brawn, and the deep quality of all-accepting fusion." [2] "Comradeship" or "manly attachment" would bring together the "blood and brawn" of the West with the "intellect" of the northeast and the "living soul" of the South. For Whitman, fusing parts into a whole not only creates one national personality out of its several regions, but also produces art, or what he calls the "alembic of a perfect poem." And "comradeship" is the glue that will tie together future generations as they fill up the West.

> [D]oubtless the child is already born who will see a hundred millions of people, the most prosperous and advanc'd of the world, inhabiting these Prairies, the great Plains, and the valley of the Mississippi, I could not help thinking it would be grander still to see all those imitable American areas fused in the alembic of a perfect poem, or other esthetic work, entirely Western, fresh and limitless—although our own, without a trace or taste of Europe's soil, reminiscence, technical letter or spirit.[3]

Whitman calls for a poem or other artwork that captures in totality what is and will be great about "inland" and "western" regions in North America, then collectively known as the West rather than today's Midwest, but the geography of these regions interests Whitman only to the degree that it provides a foundation upon which Western masculinity can develop. Fusing with others is key to the poet of adhesion, gathering millions into one; however, in doing so, he does note some distinctions, and he excludes certain groups as anathema to his fantasy of a future "America." No hint of Europe should be found in this poem, just as the West's soil has no European tradition written upon it. The perfect unifying poem should be "entirely Western—fresh, limitless." Whitman's literary manifesto, discussed in more detail later in this chapter, insists upon frank American poems about all forms of sex, so it stands to reason that a "perfect poem" ought to include language celebrating same-sex erotic friendship, called amitiveness by phrenologists in Whitman's day.[4] Whitman often claims to love and desire each and all equally, but his system, looked at carefully, distinguishes certain kinds of sexual unity from others, and favors the males-only kind.

In a short meditation in *Drum Taps* called "Western Soldiers," Whitman notices that Civil War soldiers from Illinois, Indiana, Ohio, Missouri, and Iowa are "larger in size" than troops from the North; they

> have a more serious physiognomy, are continually looking at you as they pass in the street. They are largely animal, and handsomely so.... I always feel drawn toward the men, and like their personal contact when we are crowded close together, as frequently these days in the street-cars. (Whitman's elipses 770)

Here are the qualities Whitman celebrates in his poems of "manly attachment": youth, robust Western masculinity, animal appetites in large-bodied men, and the pleasure of ogling them while in crowded mostly-male spaces. In "City of Orgies," the poet follows men on the streets whose "frequent and swift flash of eyes offering love, / Offering response to my own—these repay me, / Lovers, continual lovers repay me." The looking, the meeting, the touching, and the ecstasy of "adhesion," or affectionate feelings for same-sex friends, all produce poetry. Intimate contacts with men create a connection, and Whitman calls this connection "comradeship," which he favors over sexual contacts with women.[5]

In *Leaves of Grass*, Whitman claims to unify all individuals on the North American continent, as if absorbing them into his body. In lists, or catalogs, he labels each and every one. He considers himself to be "of" those he mentions, as if merged with them, organizing them often by their occupations: "of every hue and caste am I, over every rank and region. / A farmer, mechanic, artist, gentleman, sailor, quaker / Prisoner, fancy-man, rowdy, lawyer, physician, priest." He is "at home on" certain regions, like Canada, Vermont, and Newfoundland. However the poet is not just "of" or "at home on" but "comrade of" the robust men of the West: "Comrade of the Californians. . . . comrade of free / northwesterners, loving their big proportions" (canto 16, p. 42). With the word "comrade," Whitman carves apart a special relationship with men in California and the Pacific Northwest, supersizing them and loving their rugged, large freedoms. In Western men, particularly in their free and easy robust spirit, Whitman finds the spirit of his imaginary nation.

All Americans are to be loved by the omnivorous poet, all are to be unified, body and soul, with him, but some are loved less, and absorbed less. In a paragraph of *Specimen Days* called "The Women of the West," he writes "I am not so well satisfied with what I see of the women of the prairie cities." Based on observations he made in Denver and Kansas City during his trip in 1879, he concludes that their fashions mimic "their eastern sisters" and they are "doll-like," or derivative. Western women "do *not* have either in physique and mentality appropriate to them any high native originality of spirit or body, (as the men certainly have, appropriate to them.)" (emphasis in original, 868). With a few harsh strokes of his pen, Whitman crosses out women from the equation that will produce original poetry for the next generation of advanced and prosperous people of the American West. Not women, but "something far different and in advance must appear,"

Whitman continued, "to tally and complete the superb masculinity of the West, and maintain and continue it" (868). Comradeship and manly attachment exclusive of women or femininity captured in poetry are Whitman's answer to the question of what will gather together "the superb masculinity of the West."

Nowhere else in *Leaves of Grass* does Whitman discuss comradeship as exclusively as in the "Calamus" poems. These dozen short, free-verse poems all celebrate camaraderie. Several of them focus on the West. All the poems in the Calamus section, writes the poet, are "for all who are or have been young men, / To tell the secret of my nights and days, / To celebrate the need of comrades" (268). This need of male–male erotic affection has some distinctive forms of expression. One of the poems, called "To a Western Boy," is presented below in its entirety:

> Many things to absorb I teach to help you be an eleve of mine,
> Yet if blood like mine circle not in your veins,
> If you be not silently selected by lovers and do not silently select lovers,
> Of what use is it that you seek to be an eleve of mine?[6] (285)

The verb cluster "to absorb I teach to help" enacts linguistically a suggested space apart, where the poet/lover and the "eleve" mingle. The bold declaration "I teach" stands between two gateposts of infinitive verbs—"to absorb" and "to help"—as if Whitman stands as an educative gateway between an inner circle of comrades with "blood like mine" in their veins, and an exterior, foreign world where no like-minded lovers are selected.

The Western Boy of the title is the eleve, and if he does not "silently select lovers" as he himself is selected by lovers—if he refuses to participate in a silent erotic activity of cruising for lovers—then the poet wonders if there is any purpose in trying to be a pupil or a brother with "blood like mine," or a lover. In essence, there is a condition that comes with membership in Whitman's imagined nation. Western boys who seek to learn from the bard must meet certain standards, must "silently" select and be selected by lovers; only then will they become eleves of Whitman's. Being an eleve of Whitman's means accepting his teaching about love. In "A Promise to California," Whitman announces that he will "teach robust American love" to the men of the Sierra Nevada and coastal regions, "or inland to the great pastoral Plains, and on to Puget / Sound, and Oregon" (282). Whitman's desire to teach includes not only instruction but also absorbing and helping young men to practice his version of a citizen's duty—to select lovers, exchange lovemaking, and then depart to repeat the connection with others.

In "The Prairie Grass Dividing," Whitman's great theme, grass as a synecdoche for Americans, focuses on the Midwestern variety, that mat of food for buffalo herds and bricks for the famous sod houses in Kansas. Prairie grass is emblematic of the "superb masculinity of the West," and Whitman adds a highly homoerotic slant to the metaphor:

> The prairie-grass dividing, its special odor breathing,
> I demand of it the spiritual corresponding,
> Demand the most copious and close companionship of men,
> Demand the blades to rise of words, acts, beings,
> Those of the open atmosphere, coarse, sunlit, fresh, nutritious,
> Those that go their own gait, erect, stepping with freedom and command, leading not following,
> Those with a never-quell'd audacity, those with sweet and lusty flesh clear of taint,
> Those that look carelessly in the faces of Presidents and governors, as to say *Who are you?*
> Those of earth-born passion, simple, never constrain'd, never obedient,
> Those of inland America. (162)

Budding male sexual arousal here is palpable in the rising, erecting, commanding, looking. Like prairie grass, Western men are "coarse, sunlit, fresh, nutritious," and they also have "sweet and lusty flesh clear of taint." The poet demands of these ambitious, disobedient men "copious and close companionship."

Whitman sketches in the kind of joyous and inconsequential affection that ought to characterize citizenship in an ideal democracy. Free and easy should be citizens' relations with one another, equally deep, meaningful, intense as lovers; always and continuously cycling through comrades/lovers. Contact may be temporary, but once started, the lover is a deputy, reproducing Whitman's comaraderie in lover after lover, propagating love and citizenship like the grass on the prairie. Shirking no request for total intimacy, the poet deputizes each Western "eleve" with membership in "the most splendid race the sun ever shone on." In one of the best known of the Calamus poems, "For You O Democracy," Whitman describes how a nation of comrades will rise out of his vision of manly attachment:

> Come, I will make the continent indissoluble,
> I will make the most splendid race the sun ever shone upon,
> I will make divine magnetic lands,
>   With the love of comrades,
>   With the life-long love of comrades.
> I will plant companionship thick as trees along all the rivers
>   of America, and along the shores of the great lakes, and
>   all over the prairies,
> I will make inseparable cities with their arms about each other's necks,
>   By the love of comrades,
>   By the manly love of comrades (272)

The repeated "I will make..." or "I will plant..." suggests god-like powers to construct a whole continent, to sculpt its people, to sow companionship like seeds in fertile soil, where they will take hold, and like the grass reproduce by dividing. "By the love of comrades, / by the manly love of comrades": Whitman's ambition is large, and his partners many. He encourages his lovers to practice camaraderie with other lovers, too. In short, he promotes the goodwill generated by freely promiscuous and nonbinding physical love between men, and the best practitioners of this camaraderie are Western men.

In "I Heard It Charged Against Me," Whitman answers critics who call him an anarchist bent on destroying institutions. He denies the charge, claiming in fact to ignore existing institutions; he merely establishes a new one, "in every city of these States, inland and seaboard / ... The institution of the dear love of comrades."

Few general readers of Whitman's poems know of its foundation in a radical sex-positive manifesto in the 1856 and 1860 editions. These radical politics promote what is today called sexual promiscuity, or lover after lover, climax after climax. Although there is no indication that Whitman suffered from priapism in its clinical definition, his poetry in the early editions regularly washes his readers and its speaker with homoerotic

Illustration 13 "By the love of comrades," writes Whitman, "By the manly love of comrades" will the American nation populate the wide open spaces of the West. "Two cowpunchers posed with their horses outside a saloon in Mexico, Senora Mexico, 1910." Nitrate negative, by Erwin E. Smith. Amon Carter Museum, accession number LC-S59-470.

imagery. In "Song of Myself," the male poet describes his lover as a "Thruster holding me tight and that I hold tight! / We hurt each other as the bridegroom and the bride hurt each other." In another section of the poem, several lines conflate the sea and a solitary male swimmer into an ejaculatory splash of moisture, perhaps seawater, perhaps semen: "We must have a turn together. . . . I undress. . . . hurry me out of sight of the land, / Cushion me soft. . . . rock me in billowy drowse, / Dash me with amorous wet. . . . I can repay you."

In psychiatry, satyriasis, or Don Juanism, is an excessive and ongoing preoccupation with sexual gratification or conquest. In literature, such obsessive preoccupations are themes, leitmotifs illuminating Whitman's pansexual dogma. He promotes satyriasis in literature in order to deputize, or perhaps baptize, his "eleves." In Whitman's poems, homoeroticism is woven into the very fabric of Anglo-American culture, particularly in the imagined regions of the West.

Flush with the approval of Ralph Waldo Emerson, who found "incomparable things said incomparably well" in the 1855 edition of *Leaves of Grass*, Whitman rushed to print a second, expanded version, introduced by Emerson's letter praising his poem and an eight-page reply. This manifesto is an extraordinary document calling for a complete overthrow of conventions. It never appeared in any other edition of *Leaves of Grass*, suggesting Whitman himself backed away from its polemics.[7] Even abandoned by its writer, this statement is worth looking at because it is the earliest American document insisting upon inclusion of sex in public discourse.

For too long, Whitman says, have "bards for These States" succumbed to the "fashionable delusion of the inherent nastiness of sex; and of the feeble and querulous modesty of deprivation." (1871) No shame, cries Whitman, can ever quell the "eternal decency of the amativeness of Nature . . . / . . . / I say that the body of a man or woman, the main matter is so far quite unexpressed in poems; but that the body is to be expressed, and sex is."

In Whitman's new, revolutionary, sexualized nation, joyful sex should be the responsibility of every citizen; he celebrates sex and names its meanings deliberately, and with all, and he wants to deputize eleves to do the same. What the poems in *Leaves of Grass* deny, however, is the "long and long" tradition restricting sex to two people of opposite genders within the confines of lifelong marriage that requires sexual fidelity. Whitman's new ideology of "American" sexual identity refuses the value of monogamous intimate relations. Temporary intimate encounters between autonomous men, continuous cycling of sexual contact between citizens ought to start the love that will eventually grow to define the future nation. Being American ought to mean having multiple partners, temporary liaisons, and bonds between such lovers based on easy physicality, not emotional entanglements—regardless of gender, class, or profession.

If Walt Whitman preached promiscuity, Frank Harris lived it. By his own admission, he suffered from priapism. At age 14, he discovered that his erection did not diminish after ejaculating. Tedious it would be to count the hundreds of orgasms described in his infamous *My Life and Loves*, his sexual autobiography in five volumes. But tallying, counting, measuring, and controlling his ejaculations are exactly what Harris does in his account of his youth as a cowboy in Kansas, and his literary flowering at the University of Kansas.[8] His tireless descriptions of the maids, sailors, school chums, virgins, and married women who help him achieve his multiple orgasms have the kind of dreary cyclical self-aggrandizing sameness of a narcissist. None of Whitman's originality disguises his repetition as he records his sexual contacts with classmates in his all-boy English boarding school, with an elderly male passenger and a randy crewmember during his Atlantic crossing, and during his cattle trailing days in Texas and Kansas. Not only did he confess to his own innumerable sexual liaisons with boys, girls, men, and women, but he also published the sexual peccadilloes of his famous friends, and was embroiled in one libel lawsuit after another. It is as if Harris could not stop writing about sex. His insults included gossip about Carlyle (impotent, with a sexually frustrated virgin wife), Aubrey Beardsley (incestuous sex with his sister), Guy de Maupassant (chronic hyperexcitability of the penis), Oscar Wilde (pervert, but undeserving of punishment), and Bernard Shaw (sex addict, and proud of it).

Not only did Harris write about his persistent erections, his multiple uncontrollable nocturnal emissions, and his Casanova-like mission to seduce the wives, daughters, and female employees of his male friends, but he also poked and prodded his male friends' genitals in order to control their nocturnal emissions. Like Whitman, he was compelled to write about each and all. Harris details every sexual encounter he remembers, rendering them with the kind of naturalistic detail of a dedicated realist. In other words, Harris links his satyriasis with his literary productions:

> It was the awakening of sex-life in me, I believe, that first revealed to me the beauty of inanimate nature. A night or two later [after his first wet dream], I was ravished by a moon nearly full ... From that day on I began to live an enchanted life, for at once I tried to see beauty everywhere and at all times of day and night caught glimpses that ravished me with delight. (47)

Harris is twice ravished in a paragraph about supernal beauty in Nature, and more often ravished by multiple orgasms due to his obsessive daytime "frigging" as well as nighttime dream-induced ejaculations. Harris's awakening is both sexual and aesthetic. As a result of these dual awakenings, he starts to "enjoy descriptions of scenery in books I read, and began, too, to love landscapes in painting" (47).

Improvements, Harris soon learns, are limited. One or two ejaculations, followed by a period of abstinence, leads to aesthetic ravishment. Too many ejaculations produce mental and physical torpor. The problem with priapism, according to Harris, is that ejaculation depletes the body of energy, rendering it weak and dissolute. He notices, for example, that after multiple wet dreams in one night, he cannot measure up to the previous day's high jump mark, and his mental acuity is diminished. Calling his penis "Tommy," he explains his solution to the problem: "That night I tied up Tommy and gave myself up to thoughts of Lucielle's private parts: as soon as my sex stood and grew stiff, the whipcord hurt dreadfully and I had to apply cold water at once to reduce my unruly member to ordinary proportions" (46). This experiment works, and the next day his athletic prowess improves and his mind is sharper. Controlling his "Sex awakening" yields an another unexpected awakening: his heightened sensitivity to beauty in nature and in literature.

Harris teaches himself how to master his own body when he is a 14 year old school boy in England. When he turns 19, having immigrated to the United States and become a cowboy, he is ready to master others. In 1871, Harris met a handsome young man at a political rally in Lawrence, Kansas. "I was in cow-puncher's dress," Harris writes, having just returned from months on the cattle trail, while Byron Smith, 24, wore a stand-up white collar and a silk tie. Smith was a famed intellect, Socialist, and prodigal professor at the University of Kansas. Of their first meeting Harris "thrilled to the passion of his voice," and when Harris recites some poetry by Swinburn in order to express his belief in pantheism, Smith finishes his words. "And he wore his knowledge lightly as the mere garment of his shining spirit! And how handsome he was, like a sun-god!" (116).

In a rash gesture, Smith offers to pay for Harris to give up the cowboy life and attend the University of Kansas. Harris declines the money but agrees to attend school, and their subsequent friendship leads to numerous ravishments of mind, as Harris discovers the delights of literary scholarship, and numerous ravishments of body, as Smith discovers the benefits of penis-binding.[9] Their friendship appears to have been very intense, with Harris reporting on all manner of domestic drama in Smith's life, and becoming intimately involved with Smith's fiancée.[10] On his part, Smith instructed Harris in the classics, and twice asked the younger former cowboy to accompany him on sojourns, once to Concord to visit Emerson, and once to Philadelphia to hear Walt Whitman deliver a lecture on Thomas Paine.

Noticing that Smith grows ill "every fortnight or so" (141), Harris gets Smith to confess that "he had love-dreams that came to an orgasm and ended in emissions of seed [which] gave him intense pains in the small of his back" (142). Harris recognizes the symptoms of spermatorrhea.[11] He "went at once in search of a whipcord and tied up his unruly member for him night after night." For some days the remedy works, but a lax moment causes an inadvertent wet dream, "which brought him to misery and even intenser pain than usual" (143). Harris combines the whipcord treatment with regular horseback rides and boxing sessions, and "gradually these exercises improved his general health, and when I could tie on the cord every night for a month or so, he put on weight and gained strength surprisingly" (143). The repetition here of "night after night," and "every night for a month or so," suggests unusual devotion. Smith's "unruly member" is attached to a somewhat disobedient man, so Smith requires the discipline of a nightly repeated ritualistic binding. There is no evidence that Smith returned the favors that Harris administered, nor does Harris explain why Smith couldn't do the binding himself.

For his part, Smith leads Harris to several writers whose ideas give Harris the kind of literary ecstasy he craves as much as his sexual conquests. In 1874, Smith and Harris traveled to see Emerson in Concord but the elder philosopher did not impress Harris, who paid more attention to his traveling companion's "unruly organ" (165). Two years later, Harris traveled with Smith to Philadelphia, to hear Walt Whitman deliver a lecture. Meeting this literary giant left a lasting impression on the former cowboy.

> The impression Whitman left on me was one of transparent simplicity and sincerity: not a mannerism in him, not a trace of affectation, a man simply

sure of himself, most careful in speech, but careless of appearance and curiously, significantly free of all afterthoughts or regrets. A new type of personality which, strangely enough, has grown upon me more and more with the passing of the years and now seems to me to represent the very best of America, the large unruffled soul of that great people manifestly called and chosen to exert an increasingly important influence on the destinies of mankind. I would die happily if I could believe that America's influence would be anything like as manful and true and clear-eyed as Whitman's in guiding humanity; but alas! . . . (171)

Harris saw in Whitman the "new type of personality . . . the very best of America," a clear link between individual and nation. Whitman's best qualities, according to Harris, and therefore the best qualities of Americans, are careful speech, careless dressing, "significantly free of all afterthoughts or regrets." Americans are "manful, true, and clear-eyed." These are the qualities of Whitman and of Americans that justify their "influence on the destinies of mankind."

Harris, like Whitman, believed that sex should be the "main matter" in literature that causes aesthetic ecstasy. In Harris's words, "not only is the sexual instinct the inspiring force of all art and literature; it is also our chief teacher of gentleness and tenderness, making loving-kindness an ideal and so warning against cruelty and harshness and that misjudging of our fellows which we men call justice" (6–7). Harris and Walt Whitman share a vision of a future for Americans. Both share a vision of souls that are enlarged, expanded by encounters with beauty in art and literature, and both have male bodies whose fusion of physical "loving-kindness" and literary production creates communities—even nations. Both advocate for candidness in literature about sex, and their method requires repetition, satyriasis, or perpetual ongoing and tumescent quest for intimate sexual contact, captured in beautifully written language.

Harris and Whitman were both soundly punished for writing, if not practicing, what they preached. Prior to his sex confessions in *My Life and Loves*, Harris commanded the respect of his peers. As the incomparable editor of the *Saturday Review* in its heyday, the late 1880s and early 1890s, and as a friend of Oscar Wilde and Bernard Shaw, his moral and social eccentricities, his advocacy of anarchy, free love, and socialism in

English upper-crust society were tolerated in the same way that those of Swinebourne, Whistler, and Wilde himself were tolerated, which is to say until the elite had had enough. After Harris relinquished his editorship, and after the publication of the first volume of *My Life and Loves*, after offending, insulting, deriding, and slandering nearly everyone he knew, his reputation plummeted. H.L. Mencken was perhaps kindest when he said, after reading *My Life and Loves*, that Harris is "happily free from modesty" (xiv); Upton Sinclair was perhaps the rudest when he spat upon it and declared it "the vilest book I have ever laid eyes on: I think it absolutely inexcusable . . . poisonous!"[12]

Whitman, too, was attacked and ridiculed for his advocacy of sex. Several biographers have documented these slurs, and speculated about their influence on his revisions of *Leaves of Grass*, so it is not necessary to repeat them here, except to say that Harris himself recognized how Whitman's theory about satyriasis was the cause of the "horror and disgust" of the American public. But Harris defended Whitman's bold insistence that sex ought to be the "main matter" of American literature, in spite of any "perversion" he may have practiced: "Whitman was the first great man to write frankly about sex and five hundred years hence that will be his singular and supreme distinction" (173). It is no accident that the man who changed his name to Frank upon gaining citizenship in the United States inserted his name into a sentence about Whitman's legacy. Harris wanted to be an eleve of Whitman's. Harris felt the same about his own bold confessions, assuming that any contemporaneous objections to his challenging social norms would drop away centuries hence, and he would be celebrated in a future, less prudish, age.

The truism that great minds think alike does not extend to a comparison of writing. Harris's words about sex and literary ecstasy may echo Whitman's doctrines, but Harris's style is flat, while Whitman's is lyrical. For all the promise in his perpetual tumescence, Harris's ear for prosody is tin. His novels and stories about the American West—*My Reminiscences as a Cowboy* and *Elder Conklin and Other Stories*—never rise above mediocre, and his biographies and profiles are rightly placed in the category of failed experiments. To be fair, his biography of Oscar Wilde is still in print today, and is considered an accurate account of the vilified author's life. Harris may be one of the chief "eleves" in the school of Walt Whitman, but his literary output does not achieve the "alembic of the perfect poem" that Whitman predicted.

Nothing is known of Claude Hartland except his autobiography, *The Story of a Life*, which was published privately in 1901 by L.S. Matthews and Company in St. Louis. There is evidence that Hartland's book was banned by the post office when it was printed, in which case its intended audience—physicians who treat male nymphomaniacs—probably never read it. Just two first editions of *The Story of a Life* survive, according to *The Union Catalogue of Manuscripts*, but its brief life as a reprint in 1985 by the Grey Fox Press ensured copies are available in research libraries.[13]

Like Whitman and Harris, Hartland uses repetition of sexual encounters to make a point, not only about satyriasis but also about the criteria for inclusion in a community of men like Hartland, and the physicians who ought to stop their compulsions. Whitman "deputized" citizens of his imagined America by having sex with them. Harris conflated sexual ecstasy with aesthetic ecstasy during his awakening at the University of Kansas. Hartland repeatedly describes his sexual encounters so that doctors will study them and notice a pattern and produce a cure for what Hartland calls "my dreadful disease." He uses narrative, in other words, to define a community. "I write this little book, hoping that it may lead the physicians to give more thought to this all-important subject, and that they, in turn, may open the eyes of the laity in such a way as to check the spread of this worst of all diseases" (8). With nagging persistence, Hartland chastises physicians for ignoring his pleas for help to end his suffering, and he goads them into studying his case. In his preface he writes, "In this little volume he [the author] offers to the medical world the strange story of his own life, hoping that it may be a means by which other similar sufferers may be reached and relieved" (xiii). Unlike Whitman, who reaches out to comrades with love, or Harris whose awakenings teach "love-kindness," Hartland's text purports to be corrective. He wishes not to coerce others into having sex, but to curtail it.

In his quest for a cure, Hartland visits an asylum, but he claims the doctors there have never heard of his condition and send him away. Another physician gives him a prescription and a lecture to "resist these evil impulses." Hartland takes the pills "without any perceptible results," and soon relapses (87). He consults a "nerve specialist" named "Dr. A" who prescribes "sexual intercourse with women" (66) that Hartland tries, even though it is "the most repulsive remedy ever offered." His encounter with a female prostitute is successful only when he closes his eyes and fantasizes "so that I could not see the loathsome object beside me, . . . and turned my thoughts to a very handsome man, with whom I was madly in love in a passionate way," whereupon his "flaccid organs" rise, copulation occurs, "and when all was over, she [the prostitute] pronounced me a grand success" (67).

> I could see that my physician was greatly amused when I made my report, yet he had too much respect for my feelings to give vent to the mirth that shone in his countenance. He did not advise me to repeat the experiment, for which I was most thankful. (67)

Are we to laugh at Hartland's melodramatics, as Dr. A clearly wants to do? Is empathy for Hartland's plight with the prostitute the reason he wrote it? Are we to censor the doctor? Another physician, "middle-aged, very handsome and very intelligent," spends quite a bit of time with Hartland, "and he was never happier than when tickling, pinching, boxing and tormenting me in every way. / In this way my passions were constantly aroused" (53–54).

The subtitle for Hartland's book is "for the consideration of the Medical Community." Physicians are the designated readers of his book; they also appear as important characters. In an effect that can only be classified as ironic, Hartland even makes a "little man" he met on the streets of St. Louis, "who was affected as I am," into a physician, a love doctor:

> He spent three nights with me, and we were so much in love that we almost forgot to take our meals.
> I sought no more medical advice for I did not need it now.
> My physician was a man with a soul of love, my physic the love of his gentle soul, and I was well and happy again. (71)

Physicians, it seems, can advise abstinence, prescriptions, even sex therapy, but the cure won't work until the doctor moves in with the patient and uses his "gentle soul" as a physic. Only the last of these options is curative since it ends the need for medical advice and Hartland is "well and happy again."

With this fun-house mirroring of the audience within the text, Hartland subverts any truly scientific authority his case-study approach borrows from similar books about abnormal passions.[14] Instead, his project is literary and political, and as such his representations are all available for interpretation. Seen through the lens of irony, Hartland's autobiography is an exercise in coy pornography, titillating its readers with sex on nearly every page while justifying its prurient returns to deviant sexuality under the guise of a medical case study.

Hartland claims to have been born in 1871 in "a small railway town in the south," and lived in the "countryside," probably in southern Missouri, until he was 19 years old. His awakening sex drive torments him as he goes through school. It compels him to seduce his classmates, his teachers, and eventually, while he trains to become a teacher himself, his students. He also describes sex with his brother and his brother's friends. When he moves to St. Louis, he finds work as a tailor. His version of the city is almost entirely as a place where he finds sex with men on the streets. Hartland's list of lovers is Whitman-like in its diversity: a policeman, a minister, a teacher, a student, an actor, two physicians, a violinist, a grocery store clerk, and several men identified by physical markers such as a Van Dyke beard, a moustache, a missing finger. For all the cases he documents, none is a cowboy, a drover, an Indian, or a miner. By 1890, St. Louis may have sported the moniker as "Gateway to the West" but its street life maintained a metropolitan and cosmopolitan flair closer to the streets of New York than the lawless streets of Western boomtowns.

Still, a glance at Hartland's fantasy of his perfect lover reveals a figure that would fit very easily into the kind of masculinity Whitman associated with the West. Like Whitman, Hartland uses the list, or catalog form, and the long line to capture his ideal lover in words:

> He weighs about 185 pounds, is 6 feet tall, perfectly formed and proportioned, has a nice mustache, and knows exactly how to dress.
>
> He never wears anything showy or loud, and every article of his clothing is chosen with an eye to his own comfort.
>
> When he walks, there is not a superfluous motion about his body.
>
> His manly voice and manner are perfectly natural.

> He is not educated, and never makes the least attempt to appear so.
> He talks but little, always using the very simplest words that will convey his thoughts.
> His hands are very hard and full of corns, which he neither attempts to display nor conceal.
> Everything about him seems to say, "Here I am, just as I am. If you like me, all right; if not, then leave me alone."
> He is a man of whom I would never tire.
> He is gentle and affectionate, without being soft and silly; very passionate, but never coarse and brutal.
> He is self-forgetful in his regard for others, but never fawning in his attentions, and last, but not least, he knows exactly how often and how long to make his visits. (96–97)

This figure of easy, unaffected, working-class masculinity is an object of much desire for Hartland, arousing him frequently to paroxysms of lust. It is also a specifically literary image, endlessly repeated in popular dime novels from Street and Smith, for example, or Beadle and Adams. This picture is remarkably like the natural man Whitman impersonates in the frontispiece to the 1855 edition of *Leaves of Grass*, as well as one of the earliest known photos of him, with the open neck shirt, the frank gaze, and the slouched, relaxed attitude.

The free-and-easy "natural man" of pulp fiction was a figure that Hartland learned to love in the sentimental love stories of Bertha Clay. "I did not care for detective or Indian stories but Bertha Clay's sad, sweet tales of love filled me with keenest delight."[15] Clay's stories are almost all alike: imperiled innocents drawn to roguish men who fit Hartland's description of an ideal lover. Hartland blames Clay's books and others like it for leading him to the perils of perpetual sexual indulgence.

> When I should have been taking exercise, I was crouched down somewhere alone, dreaming, smiling and crying by turns over some sentimental love story.
> I kept this up for several years and even wrote two or three stories myself.
> From the reading of such literature I formed all sorts of incorrect notions of life. (34)

The "incorrect" notions in the books he read gave him language for the same-sex desires he discovered as a youth. In a chapter he calls "My

Illustration 14 Walt Whitman styles himself as a "rough" on the frontispiece of *Leaves of Grass* (1855). The American West, he believed, was the ideal place for the casual, frankly sexual personality of men. Walt Whitman, frontispiece of *Leaves of Grass* (1855). Steel engraving. Library of Congress accession number LC-USZ62-82784.

Conversion," covering the ages of 15 to 17, he finds so much "flowery language" in books that his "own language was becoming very flowery and, I am afraid, very ridiculous." At the same time, he was still "annoyed with a desire for my own sex, and every handsome and well developed man I saw filled me with lustful desire. I longed to clasp him in my arms, to kiss his lips; in short, to devour him but I had never yet had a chance to do so" (34). To clasp, to kiss, to devour are terms derived from the "flowery language" of novels. And just a few paragraphs later, Hartland is able to use this language to describe his first sexual encounter. It happens one night when some young men come to stay at his parent's house and "it was decided that one of them should sleep with me":

> I very timidly undressed and went to bed, and when by chance he touched me under the covers, I trembled from head to foot.
>
> He was not so timid, for we had not been in bed five minutes, when he turned toward me and boldly placed his hand upon my sexual organ, which was already erected.
>
> Upon this discovery he placed his strong arms around me and drew me up close to him, at the same time placing his cheek against my own.
>
> I could hear my heart beating, and it seemed that the blood would burst from my face.
>
> He then unfastened my clothing and his own and brought his organs and body in close contact with mine.
>
> I was simply wild with passion. All the pent-up desire of years burst forth at that moment.
>
> I threw my arms around him, kissed his lips, face and neck, and I would have annihilated him if I could.
>
> The intense animal heat and the friction between our organs soon produced a simultaneous ejaculation, which overstepped my wildest dream of sexual pleasure. (34–35)

The phrases like "wild with passion," "placed his strong arms around me," and "kissed his lips," and "annihilated him if I could" are direct descendents of the "flowery language" derived from the sentimental love stories that teach him incorrect things. Note the stylistic conventions of short sentences, short paragraphs, dramatic proclamations, and reliance on cliché. Only the "flowery language" of love stories in popular novels allows him the vocabulary to describe same-sex sexual ecstacy. This juxtaposition suggests causality: a particular kind of over indulgence in literature permits a sex act involving pounding pulses, clasping bodies, and passionate kisses.

Hartland's effeminacy would have offended Whitman, who insisted upon robust "manly attachments" in his celebration of "the superb masculinity of the West." But Hartland's passionate frenzy during sex would have appealed to the poet's aim for Literary ecstacy in poems like "One Hour to Madness and Joy" and "I sing the Body Electric." Both writers name same-sex desire, and their practice of it inspires writing. Both oscillate episodically between sexually heightened ecstasy and lyrical reflection in writing.

Like Whitman, Hartland believes that the "main matter" of literature ought to be sex. His short, often one-sentence paragraphs come one after the other, as regularly as he encounters lovers. Through this stylistic repetition, he suggests, as does Whitman by using the same technique, the regularity with which sex ought to be practiced. Physicians should notice the regularity of the event, not the individual act itself. They should note the repeated features, not the anomalous details. They should note their own participation in Hartland's "disease," and their failures unless they participate in the "disease," in which case their love becomes the cure.

For Hartland as well as for Whitman, language about male–male erotic practices produces poems and prose that imagine radical new forms of citizenship. As these writers, along with most of their countrymen, looked toward the West after the Civil War, they saw a promise of something radically new. With the tingle of the lover still with him—"I feel the hot moisture yet that he left me"—Whitman's poem tries to capture the ecstasy and its aftermath in words, naming it "comradeship" and inviting his many lovers to become citizens of an imaginary nation. Frank Harris, an immigrant cowboy turned into a literary effete, returned again and again to binding his professor's "unruly member" as if repeatedly knocking upon the door leading to literary ecstasy. A lifetime of sexual indulgences and a lifetime of reader's passions are the same thing to Frank Harris. His written confession itself repeatedly returns to sex with a metronome's cadence. Claude Hartland's text echoes Whitman's and Harris's by recording dozens and dozens of sex acts, by browbeating his readers—the physicians both within and outside his text—with his melodramatic contrition and insistence upon a cure. Look at me, he insists over and over, look at my sexual practices again and again so they can be accepted

> as the *truth* that *exists* regardless of its gravity; to think carefully over its contents, and try to devise some means of relief for the thousands whose sufferings are similar to my own; thus becoming a benefactor to society and a blessing to the world in which he lives. (99)

The "thousands" who suffer like Hartland need relief, and Hartland offers his tortured but never relinquished addiction to temporary sex encounters not only as a coded instruction manual intended to be deciphered by physicians, but also as an attempt to reach out to other men like him. The only treatment for Hartland's illness is to use love and sex to make him "well and happy again," and the doctor who discovers this will become a "benefactor to society" and a "blessing to the world in which he lives." With varying degrees of success, Whitman, Harris, and Hartland explore prohibited terrain, placing male satyriasis at the center of a new American literature that is rooted in the American West.

CHAPTER FOUR

"QUEER SECRETS" IN MEN'S CLUBS

Humor, Violence, and Homoerotic Elision in Works by Mark Twain, Bret Harte, and Eugene Field

Upon arriving by stagecoach in Carson City in 1861, Samuel Langhorne Clemens and his older brother Orion took up residence in an overcrowded boarding house, where the enterprising landlady had hung sheets of "cotton domestic" from corner to corner, subdividing single rooms into quartets to accommodate the burgeoning population of silver mining speculators. "This was the rule in Carson," Twain reported a decade later, having dropped his family name and acquired the moniker that would become so famous, "—any other kind of partition was the rare exception. And if you stood in a dark room and your neighbors in the next had lights, the shadows on your canvas told queer secrets sometimes!" The "queer secrets" pantomimed on the sheets are not the target of Twain's satire, but the sheets themselves are. "Very often these partitions were made of old flour sacks basted together; . . . the common herd had unornamented sacks, while the walls of the aristocrat were overpowering with rudimental fresco—*i.e.*, red and blue mill brands" (644). Readers of Twain will recognize his satire of aristocrats, a theme in practically all his work.

Why does Twain ignore the opportunity to skewer the "queer secrets" told in shadows upon the candlelit sheets? Male–male sex is usually the target of much derisive satire; why did Twain pass by such an obvious target? Earlier in *Roughing It*, he savagely attacks unusual forms of sexuality in his observations of Mormons in Salt Lake City. After admitting that most Mormons don't practice polygamy, Twain focuses undue attention on the few who do, mocking the practice. Wisecracks about a 72-wife-sized bed, or the problems of a harried husband multiplied beyond measure, are just a couple of his derisive jokes. His disgust takes a misogynistic flavor in his metaphor of bees, describing polygamy as "a dreadful sort of thing, this hiving together in one foul nest of mothers and daughters" (611). In the following extended attack on deviant sexuality, Twain avoids making fun of the kind that occurs between men:

> . . . some portly old frog of an elder, or a bishop, marries a girl—likes her, marries her sister—likes her, marries another sister—likes her, takes another—likes her, marries her mother—likes her, marries her father, grandfather, great grandfather, and then comes back hungry and asks for more. (611)

The accelerating repetition of the phrase "likes her" here promotes the dual meanings of *to find pleasure in* and *to resemble*, giving the feeling that once he finds what he likes, the polygamist repeats it with an addict's compulsion. As the "elder" accumulates sister-wives, his desire increases and expands, subsuming whole families as his sexual hunger grows, in an increasingly orgiastic and indiscriminate way.

Sexual excesses and homoerotic friendships are thematic in Twain's naughty lyrics, but rarely did he work them up into published literary examples. In his several ditties written for the males-only social clubs he frequented, excessive masturbation, circle jerks, gargantuan-sized penises, and foul-smelling farts are subjects worthy of literature as long as the readership excludes women. His concern for avoiding bad taste in mixed company governs his editor's pen in his published material, but his desire to make men laugh at smut governs his ribald verse, where limits of taste are directly challenged. Critics have always looked at this material askance, since it appears to have no serious literary merit. To the contrary, Twain's sub-rosa material reveals how he promoted homosocial if not homoerotic bonds as a way of consolidating privilege and power without violence. Without fear of violating a delicate, feminine reader, Twain could rev-up his satirical engines, exploring what is vile, low, and perverse.[1]

Western humor is renowned for its ricochet, its sidewinders, its sly litotes, elaborate hoaxes, and broad burlesques. Ruses and tricks are enormously entertaining, of course, but their purpose seems broader than merely tickling readers' funny bones. In the literary West, humor also elides certain tensions between men, resolving or delaying violence. The Virginian, remember, tells Trampas to smile when he calls him a son of a bitch, pulling out his gun and laying it on the poker table for emphasis. Humor functions both to mark and to measure manhood just as surely as fists, guns, or hanging ropes test masculine resolve. Two of the most successful practitioners of Western wit (indeed some claim they invented it) are Mark Twain and Bret Harte. A re-evaluation of their work reveals not only how humor sometimes turns aggressive confrontations into harmonious friendships, but also how homoerotic bonding excludes women in order to achieve and maintain exclusive privilege.

Illustration 15 Harmony between partners is an essential aspect of survival in western wildernesses. "Cowboys Rolling Cigarettes, Comanche County," photographer unknown, Kansas Historical Society accession #36-04-05-01.

Illustration 16 Making mockery of convention is a tenant of the cowboy code. In this visual burlesque, cowboy in the apron holds pride of place, while the woman and child are excluded from the fun. Cowboys dancing, flanked by band and woman with infant. Courtesy of the Texas State Libraries and Archives.

In 1895, when he died, Eugene Field was as popular as Twain and Harte, but his tales and humorous sketches of the American West never rose out of the realm of quaint or clever, and today are relatively unknown. His sentimental children's poems "Little Boy Blue" and "The Gingham Dog and the Calico Cat" still appear in nursery rhyme books, but the vast majority of his published work survives only in library archives.[2] Unearthing homoeroticism in Field's *Little Book of Western Verse* and *Little Book of Western Stories* is perhaps not as interesting as analyzing his privately printed ribaldry, where he links humor, homoeroticism, and violence in calligraphic manuscripts that he used to gain memberships to prestigious men's clubs in the East Coast cities and Europe. Its recovery here reveals how erotic codes enforce male privilege, often in the guise of humor, in well-known, well-established literature as well as then-popular-but now-forgotten texts. In Field's published works, male erotic bonding is ubiquitous in euphemism but never drawn out as a target; in privately printed works, the euphemisms drop, and the homoerotic revelry begins. For example, what is quaintly called "brotherly love" in Field's popular ballad about a mining camp restaurant, "Casey's Table d'Hôte" becomes "Rasp, roger, diddle, bugger, screw, canoodle, kife, and mow" in his bawdy poem "A French Crisis."[3] A polite locution for the affection between brothers inspires in sentimental readers the warm, easy pleasure of a love that is higher than most others; vulgarisms in a bawdy poem about anal sex would inspire in readers a guffaw, perhaps the even easier warmth of sexual arousal. Field admits to writing for both responses, and his familiarity with both brotherly love and physical male–male sex suggests a spectrum of homoerotic and homosocial discourses that has been heretofore overlooked.

Slinging words like pistols, Twain cut his writer's teeth among the rough-and-tumble newspapermen of Virginia City, Carson City, and San Francisco, where his friendship with Bret Harte was instrumental in his first literary successes. He exchanged barbs and affectionate cuffs with several rival colleagues during his days as a "Bohemian from the sage-brush," as one columnist called him in 1866.[4] Just as his river pilot days informed his writing of *The Adventures of Huckleberry Finn* and *Life on the Mississippi*, so too did his carousing with bohemians in San Francisco and journalists in Nevada mining towns inform his writing of *Roughing It*. Along with *The Innocents Abroad* and *The Gilded Age* (co-authored with Charles Dudley Warner), Twain's Western travelogue established his national reputation as a humorist in the early 1870s.

During his six years in California and Nevada, when he was writing his "lokulitems" for the Virginia City *Enterprise* and his letters to friends and family, Twain first began exploring the limits of sexual sarcasm in print. He enjoyed teasing his pious sister by claiming exaggerated sexual pecadillos. In his columns he indulged in burlesques of barrooms, theatres, and street life. Reports of his drunken rowdiness and carnal debauchery may have been greatly exaggerated in accounts written by his cronies, but all biographers agree that a kernel of truth underlies their hyperbole. As Clemens became Twain, he apparently sowed a few wild oats before marrying, and even after marriage, he occasionally enjoyed prohibited pleasures such as cigar-smoking, tippling, and off-color jokes at men's clubs.[5]

After he left California and married in 1870, Twain relied upon his wife Olivia to identify and eliminate the crass, the offensive, and the unprintable from his published work. However Olivia never saw his unpublished humor and therefore never edited his earthy burlesques and literary hi-jinx, which he produced throughout his life, including "1601, or a Fireside Conversation," "On the Science of Onanism," "The Mammoth Cod," and "The Doleful Ballad of the Neglected Lover." He shared his ribaldry with his close male friends and fellow members of all-male clubs, aiming his humor rather lower than he felt women could stand. He sought the lecherous, lewd laughter inspired by bawdy accounts of the bowels, the prick, and the cunt, using these vulgarisms to hilarious effect. In language designed to garner maximum guffaws, Twain attempted to unify male readers, creating bonds through laughter. To laugh at burlesques is to agree to suspend conventions, to agree to live in an upside-down world, where the normative symbolic order is reversed.[6] Twain admired the ribald spirit in Rabelais, Chaucer, Shakespeare, and Quixote, but it was the humor he felt was unfit for women.[7] Between men, however, with a wink, Twain celebrated male privilege by spoofing its unstoppable sexual urges and then encouraging men to practice it in groups with other men.

Bret Harte's drollery never explores the ribald territories of Twain's sub-rosa material, but his ironic reversals repeatedly idealize male erotic discourse as an alternative to violence. Harte's wit works side-by-side with catastrophic violence to first announce and then to foreclose the possibility of an idealized homoerotic union, which can only survive in the afterlife. With his triad of stories about the fictional mining camps of the Sierra Nevadas, Harte introduced fictional miscreants (the prostitute, the card shark, and the outlaw) to the pantheon of American literary heroes, imbuing them with uncommon wisdom and not a small dose of pathos. Worries about the corrupting influence of his literary ne'er-do-wells on women and children were cast aside when "The Luck of Roaring Camp" was reprinted massively in 1868. Like Cooper's descriptive passages about the American wilderness landscapes 20 years earlier, Harte's stories introduced readers in the United States and Europe to a new type of American, the mining camp misfit, who embodies the rustic charm and the folk wisdom of a survivor of wilderness. Harte's masterpiece tale of this triad is "Tennessee's Partner," which has been admired for its quirky vernacular and compressed wit. Until recently, however, few readers have commented on the way "Tennessee's Partner" slyly promotes male homoerotic partnership over male–female erotic partnerships.

Having decided in his simple and serious way that he lacked one, the Partner leaves the mountain cabin he shares with Tennessee "in order to procure a wife." He returns with a waitress, and the three live together until Tennessee elopes with her. The Partner

> took the loss of his wife simply and seriously, as was his fashion. But to everybody's surprise, when Tennessee one day returned from Marysville, without his partner's wife—she having smiled and retreated with somebody else—Tennessee's Partner was the first man to shake his hand and greet him with affection.[8]

The Partner's noncombative affection upon Tennessee's return is a breech of the masculine code; other miners in the camp expect a shooting. They are angry when the Partner shows affection for the man who stole his wife: "Their indignation might have found vent in sarcasm but for a certain look in Tennessee's Partner's eye that indicated a lack of humorous appreciation" (22).

Anyone can see the knife-edge relationship here between humor and violence, with homoerotic harmony at its center. Sarcasm from onlookers illustrates how humor potentially goads men to kill, but the Partner refuses both humorous derision and a violent solution. Instead, he welcomes the cuckold with affection, silencing satire with a look that lets his miner colleagues know that their gibes are not appreciated. With this look, the Partner says he is prepared to defend his affection for Tennessee.

Mark Twain objected to Harte's eliding this moment of violence in "Tennessee's Partner." He wrote that Harte shows no "knowledge of human nature," when he has the Partner inexplicably "*welcome back* a man who has committed against him that sin which neither the great nor the little ever forgive" (emphasis in original). Twain takes it for granted that "when old bosom friends get to hating each other, they hate like 'super-vicious devils'" (493).[9]

Indeed it is difficult to explain the Partner's lack of jealousy without attributing it to a bond of loyalty that includes homoerotic affection. One critic claims that the Partner merely delays his revenge, exacting it when he attempts to bribe the jury during Tennessee's trial for highway robbery. Revenge for cuckoldry could not be his secret motive, since the Partner shows no revenger's glee when he cuts Tennessee down from the hangman's noose, and his grief at his graveside seems real.[10]

Without Tennessee, the Partner withers and dies. His deathbed vision is of an angelic Tennessee, sober now, coming to meet him so the two can spend eternity together. Traditionalists interpret this relationship as asexual "brotherly love," a phrase that forecloses considerations of sexual aspects of their love on the grounds of an incest taboo. But the love between Partner and Tennessee, while certainly brotherly, is just as certainly erotic and therefore incestuous. They share the same wife, for a time simultaneously. The "queer secrets" their cohabitation might reveal, were they silhouetted on a screen, would almost certainly include unusual erotic practices, but such secrets are not for literature, nor life, and they are only promised in an unseen afterlife.

Harte repeatedly depicts the effects of homoerotic relations, always cutting them off from direct representation with interjections of violence, but promising them in an afterlife. "Notes by Flood and Field," "Captain Jim's Friend," "Uncle Jim and Uncle Billy," and "In the Tules" all focus on loving partnerships interrupted by violence and then continued in an idealized afterlife. "In the Tules" appeared in *The Strand* in 1895 and was widely reprinted. According to Axel Nissen, it is "[t]he most blatantly homoerotic story Harte ever wrote" (237).[11] Nissen also speculates that "In the Tules" may be Harte's coded response to the trials of Oscar Wilde, but he leaves the code undeciphered.[12] The evidence is coincidental: Harte was living in London during Wilde's trials, writing "In the Tules." Although he had met Wilde several times, and Wilde's interest in the American West had been inspired by Harte's stories, Harte wrote nothing of Wilde during or after the trials, but he surely read about them in the papers and discussed the scandal with friends. The coincidence of the trials and the authorship of "In the Tules" suggests that Harte promoted a political message in literary code: male–male erotic practices are not for the world to see, but their emotional resonance is perfectly acceptable.

"In the Tules" features a Partner-like character named Martin Morse, a country bumpkin whose bachelor hermitage on the banks of the Sacramento River is interrupted by an outlaw/murderer named Captain Jack Despard, whom Morse rescues from near drowning. The rogue spends the night, leaving once he has recovered with a promise to repay the man who saved his life, but not before Morse falls in love with him. "There is a simple intuition of friendship that is nearly akin to love at first sight," explains the narrator. "Even the audacities and insolence of this stranger [Captain Jack] affected Morse as he might have been touched and captivated by the coquetries or imperiousness of some bucolic virgin." The logic of "love at first sight" explains why Morse hovers around the tent while Captain Jack sleeps "as if he had been a Corydon watching the moonlit couch of some slumbering Amaryllis" (386).[13] Corydon is the shepherd in Virgil's second Eclogue who has fallen in love with a fellow named Alexis. Harte eliminates the part of the story where Corydon chooses Amaryllis only after Alexis rejects his love, eliding the homoerotic backstory of Virgil's version of the myth.

At the end of the story, Morse finds his roguish lover on the outskirts of a lawless mountain town, about to be lynched. Morse hurls himself upon the guards, attempting to rescue his condemned lover, but is shot. The Greek overtones of noble heroic love appear in the crowd's response: "There was something so supreme and all-powerful in this hopeless act of devotion that the heart of the multitude thrilled and then recoiled aghast at its work, and a single word or gesture from the doomed man himself would have set him free." Instead of saying the word, or making the gesture—would this word be humorous? would this gesture make the crowd laugh?—Captain Jack looks at "the hopeless sacrifice at his feet" and curses the crowd angrily. The crowd reacts violently "And Martin Morse and Captain Jack Despard were buried in the same grave" (400).

In other tales, Harte gently spoofs nonsexual male partnerships, ridiculing them but ensuring that their erotic aspects are deferred until after the story's end. The title characters of "Uncle Jim and Uncle Billy," for example, after years of sharing a cabin and mining their claim, have come to resemble one another "after the fashion of old married couples . . . it was the feminine Uncle Billy—enthusiastic, imaginative, and loquacious—who swayed the masculine, steady-going, and practical Uncle Jim" (35–36).[14] This couple shares everything—clothes, cabin, tools, views—except beds, which are bunk beds. At the story's end, having lost their claim and the scandalous riches it produced for one of them, they pool their meager resources and buy a ranch together. Using male–female marriage relations as a model for their relationship ensures that they do not deviate from the sentimental stereotype. If there are "queer secrets" being practiced in their mining cabin, they do not disresemble those that undergird the most chaste love story of the sentimental genre.

Chastity and sentimentalism are not the tools that Twain uses in representing naughty sexual stories and mock-Tudor dialogues about flatulence and copulation. Rather, broad forceful humor, delivered energetically, characterizes his sexual burlesques. Twain's earliest known spoof on sexuality appears in "The Doleful Ballad of the Rejected Lover," penned probably in 1864, the text of which has been lost but its effects were strong enough to be remembered by those who heard it. According to Biglow Paine, Twain's friend and designated biographer, "The Doleful Ballad of the Rejected Lover" is a drama for two voices, one confessing and the other consoling. Apparently Twain performed it with Steve Gillis, his roommate, for other prospectors in the Tuolumne hills during the long rainy winter months, and later in the barrooms and streets of San Francisco: "It was a wild, blasphemous outburst, and the furious fervor with which Mark and Steve delivered it, standing side by side and waving their fists, did not render it less objectionable" (Paine, chapter 50). All evidence points to the theme of this ballad being about a lover seeking sexual consolation with his best friend after being rejected by his girlfriend. The "queer secrets" of Twain's relationship with Steve Gillis are necessarily inferential, rather like the queer secrets in silhouette he saw, but did not reveal, in *Roughing It*. The missing lyrics of the "The Doleful Ballad" leave the content of this poem open, but the silhouette of "queer secrets" pantomimes the sexual side of the "blasphemous" pleasure that moved Twain and Gillis to perform it. Side by side, too, are the humor and violence of "furious fervor" and "fists" with which this hilarious camaraderie was punctuated in performance. Delight, surprise, enjoyment, laughter, and conviviality: Twain attempted to produce these effects in his off-color pieces, and rude laughter was evidence that he achieved his goals.

The balance between raucous laughter and murderous violence can be seen in the famous burlesque in *The Adventures of Huckleberry Finn*, where the King and the Duke prance around onstage, naked and painted, while the audience of roisterers prepares to lynch them; or the whipping Tom takes when Becky accidentally tears a picture of a naked man in *The Adventures of Tom Sawyer*. Again and again in Twain's published work, some form of violence exercised in the name of social control extinguishes hints at ribald eroticism.

In Twain's privately printed sub-rosa material, where readership was guaranteed male, Twain drops all hints and codes and turns his satiric spotlight full upon the phallus. Supersized male penises and their uses is the subject of "The Mammoth Cod." Told in a nursery rhyme/prayer form, the speaker thanks God for the bull, the ram, and the boar whose fornications produce future livestock, which in turn will wind up on man's dinner table. Intensifiers like "vigorous" and verbs like "packs" suggest the grim mechanics of barnyard rutting. Not for the wealthy, argues the poet, is this odious task. The poem ends with this stanza:

> Of beasts, man is the only one
> Created by our God
> Who purposely, and for mere fun,
> Plays with his mammoth cod.[15]

In a letter accompanying his poem, Twain wrote "I intended it for Sunday Schools, and when sung by hundreds of sweet, guileless children, it produces a very pretty effect" (Legman 18). The incongruity of a smutty verse sung by a choir of "guileless children" produces the laughter Twain hoped would come. Those who laugh show acquiescence to Twain's perverse order; those who frown at his impropriety run the risk of being Twain's next victims. The first response is a social leveler, aligning listener to speaker and fellow listeners, creating bonds. The second generates hierarchical social structures. The unifying laughter celebrates the lowly, the earthy, the perverse, and the taboo; disapproval creates divisions that favor highbrow prudes and sanitize the norm. Profoundly subversive to the status quo, raucous laughter momentarily suspends all rules, replacing them with a democratic community of lusty revelers.

Twain wrote "The Mammoth Cod" and its accompanying letter in 1902. In the letter, he objects to a club called The Mammoth Cod for several reasons:

> 1st. I fail to see any special merit in penises of more than the usual size. . . .
> 2nd. It is unfair for a set of men who are thus developed to arrogate themselves, superiority. . . .
> 3rd. It is unscriptural . . .
> 4th. Largeness of this organ is proof positive that it has been cultivated. . . .
> 5th. I never go where I am looked upon as an inferior. (Legman 18)

Illustration 17 Mark Twain spoofed sexual conventions in ribald ways during his stay in Nevada and California during the 1860s, but he avoided telling the "queer secrets" of miners' bedroom antics. Mark Twain, shirtless, ca. 1883. Photographer unknown. Courtesy Mark Twain Papers, Bancroft Library, University of California at Berkeley.

For each reason, Twain adds a joking commentary aimed at garnering laughter. The ironies of his objections are multiple, but chief among them is the protest against elitism. Men with larger-than-normal sex organs ought not to form a club of elites, and Twain chastises them for their cheek. His protests no doubt drew copious vales of laughter from his cronies, when it was read out loud.[16]

It is impossible to say if the members of the Mammoth Cod club were unusually well endowed, but in terms of prestige, money, and power, they were titans of American industrial, cultural, and political might. Henry H. Rogers owned the yacht where they met. The vice president of Standard Oil was also Twain's plenipotentiary and financial adviser. Laurence Hutton was the editor of *Harper's Magazine* in which Twain's writing appeared regularly. Thomas B. Reed was a former Speaker of the U.S. House of Representatives. Twain himself was at the height of his literary popularity. So to make this group laugh, to make them stoop to drunken hilarity over the privilege of being free from the work of reproductive sex, free to "play with" their mammoth cods, must have been especially liberating. Twain joins them in homoerotic circle by pointing out how God and Capitalism have conspired to grant them especially large pricks and the good sense to use them for fun. Women and workers are explicitly excluded from this pleasure. *Bonhomie* between elites is reinforced by the raucous laughter that protects and reinforces their privilege.

Looking carefully at "The Mammoth Cod" reveals its grounding in typical bourgeoisie hierarchies, depicting fornication between domestic animals as "work" in the service of man's dinner plate, while asserting that men distinguish themselves from these hard-working beasts by playing with their cods for pleasure instead of procreation. There is something about playing "for mere fun" with a phallus that separates man from beast, to whom sexual pleasure—if pleasure it is—may only serve a worker's end. A kinky political satire, Twain's poem is an indictment of class privilege from and for those who never gave up this privilege. Those at the top of the food chain exercise privilege by denying sex acts serving procreative functions, leaving such odious tasks to workers.

Twain tips his ideological hand even further in "Some Remarks on the Science of Onanism," his address to the Stomach Club in Paris in 1879. To this all-male supper club, Twain observes that a sure sign of Onanism is

"A disposition to eat, to drink, to smoke, to meet together convivially, to laugh, to joke, and to tell indelicate stories" (Legman 25). Having gathered his audience of fellow club members under the unifying term "onanists," Twain reminds his audience of several notable masturbators in literature and history—Robinson Caruso, Benjamin Franklin, Pope Julius II—and implies that in less decorous times, group masturbation was widely, if unprofitably, practiced:

> It [masturbation] is unsuited to the drawing room, and in the most cultured society it has long since been banished from the social board. It has at last, in our day of progress and improvement, been degraded to brotherhood with flatulence—among the best bred these two arts are now indulged in only in private—though by consent of the whole company, when only males are present, it is still permissible, in good society, to remove the embargo upon the fundamental sigh. (Legman 25)

Twain's grammar in this sentence is difficult to follow. How a barroom full of drunken, laughing men could track its circumlocutions is difficult to imagine. What Twain seems to be saying is that farting and jerking off in all-male circles used to be common, but "in our day of progress and improvement," only farting is permissible. Whether or not they were fully comprehensible, Twain's snaky sentences no doubt inspired loud laughter. Looked at in a sober light, one can see that Twain presumes that upper-crust society is the regulator of whether masturbation or flatulence is permitted in public, and his satire suggests a yearning for less circumspect times.

Men's clubs have long used bawdy literature and burlesque performances to promote homosocial communities defined by a common interest in earthy and satiric eroticism. Since the seventeenth century, the clubs and coffee houses of cities across Europe and North America have been instrumental in seditious antiaristocratic movements. These gatherings rarely began as explicitly political or seditious; instead, as David Shields has pointed out, the social pursuit of pleasure was usually the motive when men form clubs, and including women apparently imperiled their pleasures.[17] Under homosocial conditions, club members could receive with enthusiasm burlesques that in formal mixed-gender society would shock or silence them, and require stifling. Instead, in the unifying spirit of risibility, club members suspend the barriers against deviancies and taboo of all kinds, including male–male sex, heartily approving of them in roars of helpless laughter. Aided by inebriation, their uninhibited laughter signals their acquiescence to the ideology of the burlesque. Indeed, their "club" feeling arises from this laughter.

Eugene Field joined The Papyrus Club of Boston in 1888 as a "literary member," a status that required the applicant to write a poem and pay a reduced fee. His penned submission is called "Socratic Love," which he dedicated to the club. Before analyzing this poem, it is useful to understand a bit about the club and why a Western newspaper columnist and poet of nursery rhymes would want to broadcast homoerotic themes to its membership.

John Boyle O'Reilly founded The Papyrus Club, basing it on bohemian principles outlined in his 1885 "In Bohemia," which became a favorite

Illustration 18 Francis Wilson, left, pictured here with Eugene Field, was a flamboyant actor on the vaudeville circuit. He wrote in an April 23, 1891 letter to Field, " 'The Socratic Love' Manuscript—just tickled me to death! Now that is a possession. I have a bully lie as to how I came by it and it all reflects to your wife's credit & your everlasting disgrace." Eugene Field and Francis Wilson. Photographer unknown. Denver Public Library.

recitation piece of the drawing room set in Victorian America.[18] This anthem defining a nation of Bohemians invites "Guileless" artists and "pilgrims . . . From every class and clime and time" to find sanctuary in Bohemia, where high-toned, snobbish, moneyed society is banished. Bohemia, an imaginary nation, practices highly democratic ideals, according to O'Reilly. The elite are characterized as "the brainless heir" or "the empty heart in a jeweled breast," or snobbish society types who support Brahmin charity causes, "scrimped and iced, / in the name of a cautious, statistical Christ." For all of O'Reilly's niceties about the democratic ideals of Bohemia, most people knew it as a code word for excessive drinking, gormandizing, and sloppy bonhomie. The Papyrus Club was one such club. Patriarchs and bachelors alike gathered in various rented rooms for banquets, drinking, and poetry reading. The credo of the members of the Papyrus Club echoes the famous debaucheries of the Left Bank in Paris, but with less emphasis on avant-garde artistic sensibilities and a stronger emphasis on drinking, staying up late, and indulging in sexual excesses.

Eugene Field lived in Denver during its boomtown days, then moved to Chicago in 1883. Like Twain, Field supplemented his income with lecture tours, and while staying in Boston, he likely enjoyed his meals and drinks at private clubs like The Papyrus Club.

Today, if he is known at all, Eugene Field is known as the "poet of childhood," a sentimentalist, whose "Little Boy Blue" brought a gentle tear to the reader's eye, or whose "The Gingham Dog and the Calico Cat" was a favorite nursery rhyme. Visitors to Denver's public parks still find sculptures of Wynken, Blynken, and Nod, sailing to the land of dreams in their wooden shoe. These characters from "A Dutch Lullaby" remain in contemporary cultural memory, while the volumes of newspaper prose and poetry by Field—then widely syndicated—remains only in archives, and are forgotten by all but specialists. Field is known as the journalist who invented the "column"—that semi-editorial, partly-gossip, demi-profile, and nearly-news space in daily newspapers.[19]

Like Twain, Field wrote "respectable" prose and verse for public consumption while also writing bawdy verse for private men's clubs. Like Twain, who produced his masterpiece, *The Adventures of Huckleberry Finn*, simultaneously with his best bawdry, "1601," Field wrote his best-known work, "Little Boy Blue" at the same time as he wrote his most successful off-color poem, "Socratic Love." A comparison of the two reveals similarities in meter and rhyme, but here the likeness ends. "Little Boy Blue" is about a lonely tin solider whose playmate, a human child, goes to bed one night and dies, while "Socratic Love" is about the transformation of a beautiful Greek boy-virgin into a male nymphomaniac.

Field wrote "Socratic Love" for his membership requirement to The Papyrus Club, and its explicit lyrics about Greek style love are shocking even to those inured to such imagery. But before delving into the nitty gritty, I wish to frame his poem in a literary context. After all, Field believed he was working in the tradition of other literary greats whose immortal verses included carnal pleasures.

> Since Rabelais and Rochester and Chaucer chose to sing
> Of that which gave them subtle joy—that is to say, "the thing,"
> Why should not I, an humble bard, be pardoned if I write
> Of a certain strange occurrence which has lately come to light? (*Facetia Americana* 17)

If such literary luminaries as Chaucer and Rabelais can be pardoned their indulgence to write about "the thing," so too can Field, then a young newspaperman in Denver during its boom days, be granted a pardon for penning a smutty poem about a prodigious French whore who meets the extra-prodigiously hung American. But even more important for my purposes is Field's assumption that when Chaucer et al. "sing" about fucking, they get a "subtle joy," which the poet claims to share when he writes about deviant sex.

Like Twain, Field expresses his exaggerations in the hopes of garnering laughter from his all-male audience. However, Field was no performer, uneasy in front of crowds, so he rarely read his homoerotic verses out loud. Most people know that Twain was a consummate performer who traveled around the world giving lectures to howling applause, in front of mixed-gender as well as all-male audiences. Field, on the other hand, was a self-described bibliophile, whose pleasure came from writing and illuminating his texts, performing on the page.

It is worth analyzing a reproduction of the hand-written copy because it illustrates the care with which Field constructed this poem. Field's calligraphy may not be up to the standards of the fourteenth century, but his illuminations in green and red inks and his loosely interpreted Gothic lettering refer to this pre-Gutenberg tradition, most particularly to Rabelais.

Field's tiny script, regularized from beginning to end, suggests a schoolboy's dedication to perfect penmanship, with his emendations requiring equal precision. Furtheremore, his encyclopedic knowledge of the digestive tract, from stomach to sphincter, suggests an extended education, while his regularized rhyme and meter schemes imply a good deal of revision. In short, Field spent quite a bit of time composing and copying this poem.

The first stanza introduces Socrates, "that wise Athenian codger," and his extra-large "dodger" that swells uncontrollably whenever "Young Alcibiades" comes around. Before relating the central event of the ballade, the second stanza backtracks, informing readers of the normal sexual code among "horny Greeks":

> Now wit ye well that in those parts it was not reckoned nasty
> For sage philosophers to turn their tools to pederasty;
> The sapient Plato, whom they called in those times the master,
> Did know *a tergo*, as they say, a pretty boy bright Aster;
> And old Diogenes, who thrived by raising hell and dickens,
> Was wont to occupy all bums from pupils down to chickens,
> Whilst that revered and austere man, the great and pious Solon
> Did penetrate a Thracian youth unto his transverse colon;
> In short, it was the usual thing for horny Greeks to diddle
> This gummy vent instead of that with which the ladies piddle.

That Field here burlesques traditional forms can be seen in every compositional detail. Formal couplets, with metered marching cadence and expected rhymes, are usually reserved for stately and elevated themes; but Field desecrates them with scatological and pornographic minutia. His illumination of this stanza reveals the care with which he labored over the making of this piece.

Making a mockery of young boys who resist rape promotes a reprehensible point of view if taken seriously. But laughing at Field's burlesque, if we

Socratic Love

The story goes that Socrates, that wise Athenian codger,
Carried concealed about his clothes a rara avis bodger,
Wherewith he used, whenas he felt particularly nippy,
To ransack holes that did not appertain to his Xanthippe.
Young Alcibiades, they say, was such a pink of fashion
As to excite old Socrates into a flame of passion
Which spurred him not Xanthippe-wards, to coddle and to hug 'er,
But filled him with a violent and lewd desire to bugger.

Now wit ye well that in those parts it was not reckoned nasty
For sage philosophers to turn their tools to pederasty:
The sapient Plato, whom they called in those old times the master,
Did know a tergo, as they say, a pretty boy hight Aster;
And old Diogenes, who thrived by raising hell and dickens,
Was wont to occupy all bums from pupils down to chickens,
Whilst that revered and austere man, the great and pious Solon,
Did penetrate a Thracian youth into his transverse colon;
In short, it was the usual thing for horny Greeks to diddle
This gummy vent instead of that with which the ladies fiddle.

Illustration 19   Penning this bawdy poem for the all-male Papyrus Club in 1888, Eugene Field brought Western humor to the Boston bohemians. His singsong lyrics about Greek sexual practices must have induced raucous laughter when it was read out loud, but did the revelers realize they were the targets of the satire? Boston's educated elite males. Facsimile of "Socratic Love," ink, graphite, and watercolor on vellum, 1888. By Eugene Field. Courtesy of the Harry Ransom Humanities Research Center, The University of Texas at Austin.

permit the delight of perverse kinship with Field's bawdy fantasy, allows a connection with the author, a collusion, or what the Earl of Shaftsbury called *sensus communis*—the spontaneous shared laughter in response to a joke, laughter that opens up "free raillery," and permits speech about the unspeakable in experimental and interesting, if laughable, ways. Bawdry, ribaldry, raillery and the laughter they provoke create a temporary social context for the audacious to become familiar, for what is typically outlawed to become momentarily integrated. Laughing at smut brings what is usually taboo into everyday conversation. In this way, new ideas, deviant ideas, can be considered by the special group who laugh at burlesques.

Papyrus Club members would likely know about Socrates and Alcibiades as they appear in Plato's *The Symposium*, the elegantly composed discussion in which Socrates outlines a theory of love. Alcibiades shows up at the end of *The Symposium*, interrupting the sober conversations among philosophers, rude and drunk, and contributes his burlesque story about the origins of his love for Socrates. Scholars generally attribute Alcibiades' speech in *The Symposium* as comic relief, helpful as a metonymic device, coming immediately after Socrates' famous speech about the mystery of love and how it improves men. As a farce, Alcibiades' burlesque speech is not to be taken seriously. Indeed, his speech turns convention on its head, as he confesses he could not get the older Socrates to have sex with him no matter how blatantly he made his interest known. The orthodox Greek system of male love requires the elder man, enflamed by passion, to approach an indifferent youth.

Eugene Field reverses *The Symposium*'s burlesque reversal. Instead of the indifference Socrates feels for Alcibiades in Plato's version, Field's poem shows Socrates pursuing Alcibiades, but exchanges of wisdom for beauty are comically turned on their heads, since the youth himself appears to be unwilling to satisfy the elder statesman's lust:

> But Alcibiades was wont to make absurd objection
> When Socrates proposed the scheme of forming a connection;
> The youth conceived the childish whim that buggery was nasty—
> That his podex was for voiding dung, and not for pederasty;
> And so he grew from day to day, and his bum waxed hourly fatter
> And Socrates was nearly dead to get at that fecal matter.

For ironic effect, Field peppers this scene with references to sentimental literary conventions of his day, framing Socrates' lust as "forming a connection," for example, and depicting Alcibiades as a "youth" yielding "charms" and "blooming wealth" to an older lover. These are all euphemisms from sentimental literary sources, a parody of the asexual language of domestic (and therefore feminine) literature, besmearing its angelic discourse with a ribald sexual initiation. For the first half of the poem, Alcibiades is carefully associated with the piety and purity of true womanhood. Holding such "absurd objections" against "forming a connection" and holding an incomprehensible opinion that "pederasty" is somehow "nasty," Alcibiades is like the typical virtuous virgin putting off a rogue with hand wringing about her purity.

Alcibiades abandons his allegiance to purity very quickly, once Socrates penetrates him. Still holding a stereotypical position of womanhood, but switching from virgin to whore, Alcibiades discovers his nymphomania and regrets his previous chastity.

> Why did I not yield up my charms to Xenophon's embraces,
> As I have had the chance to do at divers times and places?
> Why not give up my blooming wealth of callipygie treasure
> To handsome Cimon's burning lust or pious Plato's pleasure?
> How would these men have gloried in my coy and virgin rectum,
> With nary thought of vagrant turd or of cundums to protect 'em!

The misogynist fantasy of a virgin transformed into a nymphomaniac is a stock feature of ribaldry from Rabelais to Chaucer, and its brutal hilarity loses none of its power when the object is a teenage boy. Alcibiades discovers in the poem that his formerly virgin orifice is, when occupied, both a source of pleasure and a ladder to higher social status. His loyalties, when it comes to using his rectum for personal gain, lampoons the historical Alcibiades' famous switching of loyalties during the Peloponnesian Wars, when he abandoned Athens for Sparta, then back again.

But the poem goes beyond merely poking fun at domesticity and Greek love: two of its central stanzas dwell upon the beauty of Alcibiades' ass. Not since Alexander Pope dwelt upon the tresses of Beatrice in *The Rape of the Lock* have so many couplets been devoted to an often-overlooked part of the human anatomy. Certainly it is the longest panegyric to an anal tract in American literature, and its deployment of medical jargon suggests that Field wrote it with an anatomy book at his elbow. In the stanza devoted to Alcibiades' ass, each line accumulates meaning, intensifying the image under high-powered magnification:

> No hair as yet profaned the vale that cleft those globes asunder—
> No hair to stay the fetid breath of borbarygmal thunder—
> No hair to interrupt the course of his diurnal ordure
> And gather from that excrement a rank dilberrie bordure.
> This sphincter was as true a band, so Socrates protested,
> As ever kept one's victuals in or passed them undigested;
> No hemorrhoids had ever marred its soft and sensuous beauty
> And on its virgin folds no prick had spent its pleasing duty;
> Like some sweet bud it nestled there, and the wind blew gently thro' it—
> Scenting that breeze, old Socrates more madly yearned to do it!

The Whitman-like repetition of "No hair" at the beginning of the stanza sets up a cadence echoed in "No hemorrhoids" and the buried "no prick" near its end, reinforcing the marching cadence of iambic heptameter. Men's clubs are famous for their ritualistic pomp, and this stanza satisfies that tradition. The poet's clear allegiance to Socratic forms of love gives this perverse ballad at least the merit of strenuous exuberance. The same might be said of Twain's "The Mammoth Cod" and its accompanying letter. Both literary burlesques appeal to readers or listeners in at least two ways: to educate and to titillate.

Eugene Field once wrote at the end of his pornographic novella *Only a Boy*, "Trusting that in the perusal of this you will be rewarded with all the pleasurable emotions that you have anticipated—that I have written nothing to burst the front buttons from the pantaloons of my gentleman friends . . . my task is ended" (61).[20] With this tongue-in-cheek denial, Field admits to encouraging erections in "you" and his gentleman friends. Such responses are merely extensions of the convivial spirits encouraged among men in the private clubs where ribald poems entertained them.

After leaving the Mississippi River, did Huckleberry Finn become a miner in the Sierra Nevadas, like Mark Twain? When he "lit out for the territories" at the end of his journey on a raft with Jim did Huck escape Aunt Sally's attempts to "sivilize" him?

Mark Twain never wrote the sequel to *The Adventures of Huckleberry Finn*, perhaps reasoning that its prequel, *The Adventures of Tom Sawyer* was enough of the young rapscallion-philosopher who has come to symbolize American manhood at its most juvenile, its most impulsive, its most morally flexible. As we have seen, Mark Twain included hints of "queer secrets" in Western towns. He hinted at unusual forms of sexuality in his novels. But in privately printed pieces, or in closed-door clubhouses, he let loose his ribald celebration of near pornographic hilarity. His obvious pleasure in the laughter produced by his pieces encourages erotic aspects of the bonds he felt for other men.

Bret Harte's queer secrets never appear in burlesques without being immediately foreclosed and then idealized. The miners of the American West, at least in Harte's stories, never practice normative desires, nor do the male partnerships violate the decorum of sentimental literature. Still, in the idealized posthumous unions between Tennessee and his partner, or Morse and Captain Jack, the erotic spark can be deciphered between the lines of catastrophe and violence.

Eugene Field's bawdy items resemble Twain's in their exuberant celebration of the lowly bodily functions and deviant sexualities. But like Harte, Field worked strictly in the sentimental vein. His *Little Book of Western Verse* was initially as popular as *The Luck of Roaring Camp and Other Stories*, as American and European readers came to appreciate the folksy contributions coming from the newspapermen of the American Western regions. However, Field's bawdy and uncensored items also reveal the ease with which male audience members could appreciate male–male sex acts without violently rejecting them.

NOTES

INTRODUCTION

1. For a good overview of the early publishing history of Westerns, see Daryl Jones's first chapter in *The Dime Novel Western* (Bowling Green, OH: Bowling Green State University Popular Press, 1978). The market for inexpensive, cowboy-adventure tales like the Buck Taylor Series, or the Young Roughriders Series, grew dramatically in the decades following the Civil War. Companies like the House of Beadle and Adams, the leader in the market, or its successful competitor Street and Smith, prospered by churning out hundreds of five-cent weeklies, yellow backs, Ten Cent Novels, and penny pamphlets every year. Pulp (low-quality paper) was cheap, and the recently invented steam-rotary press reduced production costs significantly. And the sales figures are impressive: A first printing of sixty to seventy thousand often went through ten or twelve editions in a single year, eventually selling more than six hundred thousand copies and being translated into half a dozen languages (Jones 5). There were probably more readers than the sales figures suggest, since the inexpensive paperbacks were frequently passed from hand to hand until they were literally read to pieces.
2. See Ben Merchant Vorpahl's *My Dear Wister: The Frederic Remington—Own Wister Letters* (Palo Alto: Stanford University Press, 1972), p. 303.
3. "Frontier" is a widely contested term. Traditionally when applied in Colonial and Early American contexts, "frontier" means the region outside settlements along the Atlantic territories of North America. In the nineteenth century, Anglo-Americans use the term "frontier" to mean an amorphous line extending from the banks of the Mississippi and Missouri Rivers westward. In symbolic terms, "frontier" meant

a location where epic encounters between opposing forces occur—civilization and wilderness, cowboy and Indian, familiar and foreign. Frederick Jackson Turner famously announced that the "first period of American history" ended in the 1890s when the frontier—that rolling line advancing from East to West—reached the Pacific Ocean and the "sea to shining sea" wish envisioned by Thomas Jefferson came true. The truest American character, according to Turner, was shaped in this imagined place he called "frontier" and his essay mourns its loss in elegiac terms. William R. Handley outlines the literary perspectives in Turner's thesis in *Marriage, Violence, and the Nation in the American Literary West* (New York: Cambridge University Press, 2001), pp. 43–66. See also Patricia Nelson Limerick, *Something in the Soil: Legacies and Reckonings in the New West* (New York: W.W. Norton & Co., 2000).

4. Ellison, Ralph. "Change the Joke and Slip the Yoke," *Shadow and Act*. New York: Random House, 1964, p. 51.
5. Feidler, Leslie. "Come Back to the Raft Ag'in, Huck Honey!" *The Partisan Review*, XV:6 (June) 1948: 664–671.
6. Historians have pinpointed the moment when "the homosexual" was invented: Karl Westphal worte an article in 1870 called "Die Konträre Sexualempfindung (Contrary Sexual Sensations)." See Michel Foucalt's *The History of Sexuality*, Vol. I (New York: Random House, 1978). Popular usage of this specialized term didn't emerge until the 1920s.
7. See Christopher Looby's " 'Innocent Homosexuality': The Fiedler Thesis in Retrospect," *The Adventures of Huckleberry Finn* (New York: Bedford Books, 1995), 535–550.
8. Michaels, Walter Benn. *Our America: Nativism, Modernism, and Pluralism*. Durham: Duke University Press, 1995.
9. Richard Slotkin's *Gunfighter Nation*, and Ogden Nash Smith's *Virgin Land* are excellent sources, but they avoid analyzing the cowboy's sexual and erotic histories in this literary tradition.
10. The chapter is called "A Reminiscent Night," pp. 70–83. Although he massaged the truth considerably, Andy Adams is credited, along with Charlie Siringo's *A Texas Cowboy* (1883), with representing the authentic cowboy experience in his autobiography. J. Frank Dobie,

e.g., claims that *The Log of a Cowboy* is "a just and authentic conception of trail men." The demands for realism in the genre were high; see Richard Dorson's *America in Legend* (New York: Pantheon, 1973) for testimonial evidence about such demands from fans of Westerns (129–131).

11. Analogies between breeding cattle and human sexuality are common in cowboy vernacular, as Blake Allmendinger has pointed out in *The Cowboy: Representations of Labor in an American Work Culture* (New York: Oxford University Press, 1992), pp. 48–82.
12. Tompkins, Jane. *West of Everything: The Inner Life of Westerns.* New York: Oxford University Press, 1992.
13. Clark, Badger C. *Sun and Saddle Leather with Additional Poems.* Boston: R. G. Badger, 1917.
14. Bruce Seiberts. *Nothing but Prairie and Sky: Life on the Dakota Range in the Early Days.* Norman, OK: University of Oklahoma Press, 1954.
15. These synonyms for "penis" come from "A French Crisis" by Eugene Field in *Facetia Americana* (Priv. Printed, 1935), p. 17.
16. These views are promoted by R.W.B Lewis in *The American Adam: Innocence, Tragedy and Tradition in Nineteenth Century Literature* (Chicago: University of Chicago Press, 1955), Harry Levin (*The Power of Blackness: Hawthorne, Poe, Melville.* New York: Knopf, 1970), and Leo Marx (*The Machine in the Garden: Technology and the Pastoral Ideal in America.* New York: Oxford University Press, 1999).
17. Faderman, Lillian. *Surpassing the Love of Men: Romantic Friendship and Love between Women from the Renaissance to the Present.* New York: Morrow, William & Co., 1994.
18. Philip Durham and Everett L. Jones, *The Negro Cowboys.* Lincoln: University of Nebraska Press, 1965.
19. Clifford Westermeier in "The Cowboy and Sex" (in *The Cowboy: Six Shooters, Songs and Sex*, ed. Charles W. Harris and Buck Rainy. Norman: University of Oklahoma Press, 1976, pp. 98–105) limits his discussion about homosexuality and cowboys to gay male pornography produced in the 1970s in films and paperbacks. These productions feature the cowboy as a fetish object. "Long before the movies

sullied the cowboy by casting him as an anti-hero, sadist, sodomite, and homosexual, the pornographers found that here was a ready-made sex symbol—a man's man with all the equipment to satisfy the desire and differences of readers and audiences" (101).

ALL-MALE QUEER INTERRACIAL FAMILIES IN THE WILDERNESS

1. John Cawelti in *The Six Gun Mystique* (Bowling Green, OH: Bowling Green University Popular Press, 1984) also argues that Cooper is the first writer of Westerns because he brings together three character types into a Western landscape (41): the townies, who represent civilization; the hero, who is a middle figure; and the savages, who represent destruction and/or chaos (Indians or outlaws).
2. Henry Nash Smith in *Virgin Land: The American West as Symbol and Myth* (Cambridge: Harvard University Press, 1950) argues that Natty Bumppo is the archetypal Western hero, based loosely on the legend of Daniel Boone. But Smith got it wrong when he said that Bumppo surmounted his " 'arthy" origins and elevated himself to be worthy of the aristocratic women who fall in love with him. In fact, Leather stocking rejects or is rejected by every white woman he shows an interest in, regardless of whether or not he elevates himself. In today's terminology, he is a failed heterosexual.
3. See Danhnall Mitchell, "Acts of Intercourse: 'Miscegenation' and Three 19th-Century American Novels," *American Studies in Scandinavia*, 27 (1995): 126–141.
4. All citations from Cooper's *Leatherstocking Tales* come from The Library of America edition of *The Leatherstocking Tales*, published in two volumes, which include all five novels. Hereafter referred to parenthetically as LT I (*The Pioneers, The Prairie, The Last of the Mohicans*) and LT II (*The Pathfinder* and *The Deerslayer*).
5. Marriage bonds in nineteenth-century America were reserved for an elite group who put much effort into insisting that others practice no marriage rituals at all. Slaves could not marry each other; Native Americans and Mestizos could not marry Anglos, Mormons established

a radical outpost in Utah where polygamy was legal, and California was associated with divorce from the moment it was admitted to the Union in 1854. See Glenda Riley's *Building and Breaking Families in the American West* (Albuquerque, NM: The University of New Mexico Press, 1996).

6. Queer theory has generated quite a lot of discussion about the triangulation of desire, but this geometrical structure does not adequately describe the way desire is distributed in *The Leatherstocking Tales*. Eve Kosofsky Sedgwick's *Epistemology of the Closet* (Berkeley, CA: University of California Press, 1990), and Rene Girard's *Deceit, Desire and the Novel: Self and Other in Literary Structure*. Trans. Yvonne Freccero (Baltimore: Johns Hopkins University Press, 1975) have outlined this pattern in English and American literature of the nineteenth century, where two men express their prohibited desire for each other in a common desire for a woman, where homosocial rivalry is a substitute for homoerotic desire, preserving male privilege. Leatherstocking's desire to copulate with Indian women implies an unsound mind, an equation that forces him to keep his desire in check. Desire for Chingachgook is permissible. This structure of desire is less a triangle than it is a parallelogram, where Leatherstocking's stated desire for his "fri'nd" is a ghost of his desire for a squaw.

7. R.W.B. Lewis explains the frontier hero's sexuality by eliminating it. As an "American Adam," Cooper's heroes enjoy a pre-lapsarian freedom from sexual practices; he is a neutered character whose "timeless and sturdily innocent" friendship with Chingachgook is "fresh, free, and uncluttered."

8. According to Richard C. Trexler in *Sex and Conquest: Gendered Violence, Political Order, and the European Conquest of the Americas* (Ithaca, NY: Cornell University Press, 1995), in the mind of a Delaware chief, male clothing sometimes meant nudity, while female clothing always meant covering the body.

9. John Seelye believes that "the habit of forcing landscape and its aboriginal inhabitants . . . into acceptable aesthetic arrangements" is at the very heart of the imperialist's project. See "Captives, Captains, Cowboys, Indians: Frames of Reference and the American West," *American Literary History*, 7:2 (Summer 1995): 304–319.

10. All quotes from *The Pilot* and *The Red Rover* come from a volume called *Sea Tales* (New York: The Library of America, 1983), parenthetically referred to as ST. All quotes from *The Two Admirals* (Albany: State University of New York Press, 1990), are parenthetically referred to as TTA.
11. Although never a slave, Scipio Africanus can be compared to Nebachadnezzar in Cooper's *Afloat and Ashore* (1844), whose attachment to his master is an uneasy mixture of "the pride of a partisan, the solicitude of a parent, and the blindness of a lover".
12. See Mitchell, p. 126.
13. In a test of loyalties, Admiral Bluewater abandons his Jacobite leanings, at the last minute, throwing the weight of his fighting force behind his Whig-supporting partner Admiral Oakes, essentially for sentimental reasons, indicating how Cooper favors the strength and primacy of masculine affection over political loyalty.
14. Richard H. Ballinger, "Origins of James Fenimore Cooper's *The Two Admirals*," *American Literature*, 20 (March 1948): 24–29. See also Donald A. Ringe's "Historical Introduction" to TTA, p. xviii.
15. The deathbed scene lasts for several chapters, during which a hasty marriage and a change of wills facilitates a plot resolution and restores a seemingly low-born Mary Dutton to her rightful place among British aristocrats, and her husband, the admirals' adopted son. My focus on the kiss between Dick and Oakes illustrates their intimacy. The protracted deathbed scene establishes their parentage over the main characters in this book.
16. The lack of gender dichotomy is remarkable in this relationship. Cooper gives no hint of which Admiral is the heroine, and the clues in the text are decidedly ambiguous. When Oakes writes Dick a note asking him to come ashore, he includes a postscript that speaks his mind "like a woman" (159). He cooks rather well, and he is stickler for details, while by contrast Dick Bluewater affects a Byronic disregard for temporal details like good food, and he bends the rules when it suits him (164–165). The stereotypically more feminine character, Oakes, slightly outranks the more stereotypically masculine Bluewater, whose secondary status does not temper his passion for his friend.

17. *The Globe*, May 19, 1843, p. [3], Reprinted from the *Southern Patriot*.
18. I am indebted here to Walter Benn Michael's notion of male nonreproductive families as national ideals in the literature of Modernism in *Our America: Nativism, Modernism, and Pluralism* (Duke University Press, 1997).
19. To "monkey around" in late-twentieth-century slang has explicitly sexual overtones. Quinn cites evidence that nineteenth-century Americans understood the word to mean anal intercourse between two or more men. See Quinn 325–326 and n. 121, pp. 310–311.
20. According to Walter L. Williams's *The Spirit and the Flesh: Sexual Diversity in American Indian Culture* (Boston: Beacon Press, 1992), when a young child of almost all Native American tribes chooses a feminine object over a masculine object in the "berdache" ritual, the man will become a shaman, a two-spirited spiritual leader, a "she-man" or "man-woman." Among other privileges, a berdache enjoys sexual marriages with men of the tribe.
21. Leavy, Barbara Fass. *In Search of the Swan Maiden: A Narrative on Folklore and Gender*. New York: New York University Press, 1994.

REHEARSING AND RIDICULING MARRIAGE IN *THE VIRGINIAN* AND OTHER ADVENTURE TALES

1. Wister spoofs the phrase "proposing marriage" by including among its meanings "to copulate" in the following passage from his 1888 journal: "This day two mink [*sic*] came tearing into camp together, all among the pots and kettles while all but I were at dinner. They were proposing marriage on the spot—and therefore ignored all other things. Result—she escaped, his skin hangs on a tree" (*Journals* 75).
2. Wister, Owen. *The Virginian*. New York: Penguin Classics, 1988, pp. 384–385. Subsequent references appear parenthetically.
3. Andy Adams, *A Texas Matchmaker*. Boston: Houghton Mifflin, 1903, p. 281. Subsequent references appear parenthetically.

4. Several critics have analyzed the implied homoerotic relationship between Steve and the Virginian: among them Blake Allmendinger (*Ten Most Wanted: The New Western Literature*, New York: Routledge Press, 1998), Jane Tompkins (*West of Everything: The Inner Life of Westerns*, New York: Oxford University Press, 1992), and William R. Handley (*Marriage, Violence, and the Nation in the American Literary West*, New York: Cambridge University Press, 2002).
5. Here is the full text of the poem that appears in Wister's 1983 journal (reprinted in *Owen Wister Out West: His Journals and Letters*, ed. Fanny Kemble Wister, Chicago: University of Chicago Press, 1958, pp. 253–254):

> There are some things we say but must not hear;
> There are some things we do yet cannot know;
> Our clean starched image prinked up thus and so
> Utters "Mama! Papa!" and walks so near
> The Life, 'twere monstrous not to hold it dear;
> No vandal shall intrude to aim a blow
> And mar our mannequin, and overthrow
> The pious clock-work we have toiled to rear.
>
> Immortal ostrich! Anglosaxon bird!
> Bury your head in print so none shall see
> Your large wise body looming through the sham.
> Let not reality be ever heard;
> It is unfit and shocking; but let me
> Meanwhile sit in some corner and say damn! (O sugar!)
>
> Yes, I'm aware your daughter cannot read it;
> I don't forget your piano stands on limbs.
> Life's so indelicate, we have agreed it
> Must be concealed by fig leaves and by hymns.
> Sculpture's so bare, and painting so illicit,
> And poets unconventional at best;
> Give Art a chance and Art will never miss it;
> Art has a craving to parade undressed.

6. "Hank's Woman" was removed from *The Virginian* late in the process of writing the novel. It was first written and published in 1891, Wister's

earliest cowboy story, and later revised for his 1890 collection, *The Jimmy-John Boss*.
7. See Barbara Welter's article, "The Cult of True Womanhood: 1820–1860," in *Locating American Studies*, ed. Lucy Maddox (Baltimore, MD: Johns Hopkins University Press, 1999).
8. See Lee Clark Mitchell's *Westerns: Making the Man in Westerns and Film* (Chicago: University of Chicago Press, 1996).
9. The story the Virginian tells the narrator in "Hank's Woman" is gruesome. Hank is an ornery, short-tempered drunk who marries a devout Austrian Catholic whose English isn't very good. Her devotion to her crucifix enrages Hank, so he shoots the relic, whereupon Willomene buries a hatchet in Hank's brain. While trying to dump his body into a ravine, she slips, falls, and dies.
10. John Seelye does a good job of outlining the erotic interlude between the narrator and the Virginian during this camping scene in his introduction to *The Virginian* (New York: Penguin, 1988, pp. vii–xxxiii).
11. Barbara Will's article, "The Nervous Origins of the American Western" (*American Literature*, 70.2 [June 1998]: 293–316) discusses Wister's diagnosis of "nervousness" and the Western cure. For analysis of the West/Wister letters, see William Handley's *Marriage, Violence, and Nation in the American West* (New York: Cambridge University Press), pp. 80–81.
12. Michael Warner is right when he identifies a major concern of Irving, Cooper, and Lamb was the figure of the bachelor poised on the brink of modernity. See "Irving's Posterity" (*ELH*, 67.3 [2000]: 773–799).
13. This dichotomy between cloyingly feminine domesticity and the healthy masculine air of the West is a slogan often used to recruit "rough riders" and other macho enforcers of U.S. imperialistic practices in the late 1800s. This theme is richly chronicled by Richard Slotkin's *Gunfighter Nation* and his earlier *Regeneration through Violence: the Mythology of the American Frontier 1600–1860* (Middletown, CT: Wesleyan University Press, 1973). G. Edward White has also explored the dichotomy between East and West in American settlement ideology in *The Eastern Establishment and the Western Experience: The West of Frederick Remington, Theodore Roosevelt, and Owen Wister* (New Haven: Yale University Press, 1968).

14. Several good histories of homosexuality in America exist. John D'Emilio and Estelle Freedman's classic *Intimate Matters: A History of Sexuality in America*, 2nd edition (Chicago: University of Chicago Press, 1997) and Jonathan Ned Katz's *Gay American History* (New York: Meridian, 1992) are good sources of documentary evidence, although neither focuses upon the American West during the nineteenth century, nor do they include literature as evidence. D. Michael Quinn's superlative *Same-Sex Dynamics Among Nineteenth-Century Americans: A Mormon Example* (Chicago: University of Illinois Press, 1996) uncovers major new historical sources from nineteenth-century records of the Church of the Latter Day Saints. He classifies his evidence into groups according to same-sex behaviors, such as homotactile and homomarital, and same-sex cultures, such as homoromantic, homoenvironmental, and homopastoral. His analysis of photographs of sports teams in all-boys schools suggests that images taken before 1900 show the kind of easy touching permissible in the nineteenth century, while post-1900 team pictures show less touching and more space between bodies (see illustrations between pp. 230 and 213). James Creech theorizes literary codes about nineteenth-century homoeroticism, *Closet Writing / Gay Reading: The Case of Melville's Pierre* (Chicago: University of Chicago Press, 1993), but doesn't address Westerns.
15. David Deitcher studies the uncertainty of motive in the gestures captured by photographs of men together in his wonderful *Dear Friends: American Photographs of Men Together, 1840–1918* (New York: Narry N. Abrams, 2001).
16. See Seelye, p. xix.
17. Philip Warne surprised his editors at Beadle and Adams by being black. Having never met the man, having hired him from afar, and having conducted all their business through the mail, they never realized he was "a New Orleans Negro" who made his living in the years after the Civil War by writing action-adventure Westerns and stories for the New York City firm. See Johanssen's biography.
18. Ridge, John Rollin. *The Life and Adventures of Joaquin Murieta, the Celebrated California Bandit* (1854). Norman, OK: University of Oklahoma Press, 1955.

19. See Robert K. Martin's excellent *Hero, Captain, Stranger: Male Friendship, Social Critique, and Literary Form in the Sea Novels of Herman Melville* (Chapel Hill: University of North Carolina Press, 1986).
20. Herman Melville, *Billy Budd, Sailor*, The Library of America edition, 1984, p. 1353.
21. Annie Proulx's short story, "Brokeback Mountain," caused a sensation when it appeared in *The New Yorker* (Oct. 13, 1997) because it imagines the sexual and loving affection between two Westerners both before and after one of them marries and has children. Ang Lee's filmed adaptation is scheduled to appear in 2005.
22. Pilgrim, Thomas (C.J.). *Live boys, or, Charley and Nasho in Texas: a narrative relating to two boys of fourteen, one a Texan, the other a Mexican: showing their life on the great Texas cattle trail and their adventures in the Indian territory, Kansas, and Northern Texas: embracing many thrilling adventures taken down from Charley's narrative / by Arthur Morecamp*. Boston: Lee and Shepard Publishers. New York: Charles T. Dillingham, 1879.
23. Cooper claimed that his descriptions of the wilderness in the first four *Leatherstocking Tales* came from his memory as a boy in the remote regions of upstate New York. His descriptions of the West in *The Prairie* are derived wholly from secondary sources.
24. See Albert Johannson, *The House of Beadle and Adams*, Vol. 2 (Norman: University of Oklahoma Press, 1950), p. 289.
25. Siringo's *A Texas Cowboy* hints at no homoerotic themes, but he did write down the lyrics of a song, "A Jolly Cowboy," that begins "My lover is a cowboy." Siringo apparently learned this tune from a young cowboy named L.S. Kidd. There is no notation that requires the singer to be female.
26. For a good discussion of the kind of robust masculinity expected of Harvard graduates during the late nineteenth century, see Kim Townsend's *Manhood at Harvard: William James and Others* (New York: W.W. Norton & Co., 1996).
27. *The New York Times*, November 24, 1871, vol. XXI, no. 6296, p. 5, col. 2. The obituary in *Appleton's Journal* explains his desire to go West this way: "Last spring, Lieutenant Wheeler, of the army, who was

about to explore Arizona at the head of a Government expedition, requested us to appoint some competent young writer to accompany the party as a representative of APPLETON'S JOURNAL. We offered the position to Mr. Loring, who accepted it with the greatest eagerness and enthusiasm. Such an expedition exactly suited his romantic and adventurous disposition, and Lieut. Wheeler and the rest of the party were delighted with the acquisition of so bright, buoyant, handsome, and gifted a comrade" (December 9, 1871, p. 666).
28. *Appleton's Journal*, August 19, 1871, p. 182.
29. Douglass Shand-Tucci believes this omission indicates "a certain discomfort about *Two College Friends*" on the part of his Harvard classmates. See "A Gay Civil War Novel Surfaces," *The Harvard Gay and Lesbian Review*, III. 2 (Spring 1996): 9–12.

AMERICAN SATYRIASIS IN WHITMAN, HARRIS, AND HARTLAND

1. The entire interview appears in Walter H. Eitner's *Walt Whitman's Western Jaunt* (Lawrence, KS: The Regents Press of Kansas, 1981), pp. 83–85. As Eitner points out, it is likely that Whitman wrote this interview himself, as similar "press releases" he authored appeared in other Western newspapers during his trip to St. Louis, Kansas City, Lawrence, and Denver.
2. All citations of Whitman's poetry and prose come from *Walt Whitman: Complete Poetry and Collected Prose*, 1871. Reprinted. ed. Justin Kaplan (New York: The Library of America, 1982), p. 2095.
3. Quoted in Gay Wilson Allen's *The Solitary Singer: A Critical Biography of Walt Whitman* (New York: Macmillan, 1955), pp. 487–488, originally from Whitman's *Complete Works*, 1904, vol. VIII, p. 48.
4. Michael Lynch's " 'Here is Adhesiveness' " helps to make the distinction between the procreative and the non-procreative sex drives in nineteenth-century vernacular of the pseudoscience called phrenology. According to Lynch, Whitman applies the meaning of the words *amativeness* ("instinct for generation") to the Children of Adam section, and *adhesiveness* ("instinct for attachments") to the Calamus section.

The distinctions belong to the phrenologists who divided instincts for procreation and same-sex affection into separate areas of the brain. Michael Lynch " 'Here is Adhesiveness': From Friendship to Homosexuality," *Victorian Studies* 29 (Autumn 1985): 67–96. Lynch traces the word to Franz Josef Gall's use of *Anhanglichkeit* in his early work on the science of phrenology. Lynch explains that phrenologists located the adhesiveness "bump" at the back of the head, over what is today called the hypothalamus gland. The largest "bumps" indicated excessive passion for persons of the same sex. In a striking coincidence, a recent study suggests that homosexuality is "caused" in men by a "smaller than normal" hypothalamus gland (*The New York Times*, August 15, 1991). From large bumps in the 1840s to small glands in the 1990s: the scientific search for the "cause" of homosexuality proceeds apace.

5. Whitman claims equal affection for all of his lovers, but careful analysis reveals meaningful differences divided along gender lines. In general, the poet of the early editions of *Leaves of Grass* enjoys sex with women in order to spawn "sons and daughters fit for these / States," while he enjoys sex with men in order to deputize his lovers directly as citizens of his idealized, poeticized "America." Particularly in the "Children of Adam" poems, with women he doesn't linger, always moving quickly to the next lover in a kind of frenzied rush. Consider the pronouns bracketing "you woman" within the bars of a twice repeated "I":

> It is I, you women, I make my way,
> I am stern, acrid, large, undissuadable, but I love you,
> I do not hurt you any more than is necessary for you,
> I pour the stuff to start sons and daughters fit for these
> States, I press with slow rude muscle. (259)

His cursory "but I love you" seems an afterthought as the poet presses in, imposes his concupiscence upon "you women" as if his duty is the same as a breeding sire. Receptivity is not a consideration in his task, and there is very little evidence that duties include care taking of his progeny. Poems of maternity, or even of the domestic sphere, are relatively few in Whitman's opus, while poems of the fleeting erotic and temporary sexual encounter, often when both poet and lover are male, come with the regularity of ocean waves.

6. Whitman uses an Americanized version of *élève* without the accent marks, retaining the French meaning (pupil, student, and cadet) as well as its American slang meaning (supernatural beings of the woods like those found in "Rip Van Winkle," pre-Christian figures of myth).
7. Michael Moon's *Disseminating Whitman: Revision and Corporeality in* Leaves of Grass (Cambridge: Harvard University Press, 1991) tracks Whitman's revisions between 1855 and 1867, which reflect his culture's changing view of the human body.
8. *My Life and Loves* covers far more than the roughly six years when Harris was working the cattle trails, living in Lawrence, and attending the University of Kansas. However, since my focus is upon homoeroticism in literature focusing on cowboys and the American West, I have excluded a full discussion of the parts of Harris's autobiography devoted to his European years.
9. Harris writes that Balzac purportedly could not write for "at least a fortnight" after a wet dream (224). Based on the assumption that ejaculation depletes the creative drive, Harris concludes that Shakespeare was probably of poor virility in order to produce such masterpieces.
10. Kate Stephens denied their intimacies. See her *Lies and Libels of Frank Harris* (New York: Autigone Press, 1929).
11. John S. Haller and Robin M. Haller in *The Physician and Sexuality in Victorian America* (Urbana, IL: The University of Illinois Press, 1974) affirm that Harris's view derives from a contemporaneous scientific theory that ejaculation depletes physical and psychic energies. In this theory, ejaculate is considered to be highly concentrated blood that has been filtered through the brain, traveled down the spinal column, into the scrotum, and out the phallus during an orgasm. Two weeks appeared to be the optimum interval between ejaculations, during which time men suffered from dissipation while their bodies refined more blood to replace the load. Excessive ejaculations in any form (nocturnal emissions were of great concern) essentially meant a man's brains were being squirted out, with the eventual result of lunacy.
12. See Vincent Brome's *Frank Harris: The Life and Loves of a Scoundrel* (New York: T. Yoseloff, 1960), p. 193 and Gallagher's Introduction to *My Life and Loves* by Frank Harris, p. xi.

13. The Grey Fox Press edition of 1985 is not scholarly. Its editor, C.A. Tripp, made "silent corrections of perhaps a dozen minor typographical errors."
14. James Gifford's *Dayneford's Library: American Homosexual Writing, 1900–1913* (Amherst: University of Massachusetts Press, 1995) provides the only serious literary scholarship done on *The Story of a Life*. He assumes "Claude Hartland" is a pseudonym. Hartland was chosen, perhaps, because it referred to both his region of origin as well as "symbolic emotional nexus" (49). Gifford classifies Hartland's case-study approach to his chronicle of sexual conquest, as modeled upon Havelock Ellis's and John Addington Symmond's *Sexual Inversion* (1897) and Krafft-Ebin's *Psychopathia Sexualis* (1886). It is impossible to know whether the author had read these books, but Gifford's interpretation seems right: Hartland combines pseudoscientific analysis to what he called "My abnormal passion," with hardboiled naturalistic flourishes reminiscent of Stephen Crane or Frank Norris.
15. Bertha Clay is the pseudonym for at least three authors in the period that Hartland is devouring her texts. The most likely is "Bertha M. Clay" (1865–1922) who wrote more than 30 love stories for Street and Smith in the late 1880s—the early 1900s, with titles like *In Cupid's Net* (1886) or *Violet Lisle* (1892).

"QUEER SECRETS" IN MEN'S CLUBS

1. Twaniana is replete with stories of how Olivia Langhorne Clemens, or "Livy" to Twain, edited his manuscripts while he was alive, and excised objectionable material. Apparently, she never saw his sub-rosa writings.
2. Recently, Lewis O. Saum published *Eugene Field and His Age* (Lincoln: University of Nebraska Press, 2000), which does a remarkable job of recovering the local political references in Field's columns.
3. Another of Field's compositions is a ballad called "Casey's Table d'Hôte." The speaker of the poem is an elderly man remembering his good times as a youth in a mining camp on Red Hoss Mountain. In thinking about Casey's "restauraw," the speaker is covertly thinking

about his lost homoerotic love. In the last stanza, the speaker feel "a yearnin' in my buzzam" and his eyes well up with tears when he recalls his partner

> ... a-sleepin' way out west,
> With Red Hoss Mountain huggin' you close to its lovin' breast,—
> O, do you dream in your last sleep of how we use to do,
> Of how we worked our little claims together, me 'nd you?

The dead partner's dream is too painful for the speaker to bear remembering:

> But, bein' how a brother's love aint for the world to know;
> Whenever I've this heartache 'nd this chokin' in my throat,
> I lay it all to thinkin' of Casey's tabble dote."

The charm of this poem is the scrappy old speaker's attempts to resist the heartache by remembering not the secret of "a brother's love," but the Irishman's restaurant.

4. See Nigey Lennon, *The Sagebrush Bohemian: Mark Twain in California* (New York: Paragon House, 1990). "Sagebrush" connotes the high desert regions where uncultivated hooligans come from, while "bohemian" connotes debauchery.
5. Andrew J. Hoffman documents Twain's erotic relations with at least four journalists with whom he shared quarters between 1861 and 1865. See "Mark Twain and Homosexuality," *American Literature*, 67.1 (March 1995): 23–49.
6. Mikhail Bakhtin argues this point cogently in his *Rabelais and His World*. (Trans. Helene Iswolsky. Cambridge, MA: The Massachusetts Institute of Technology Press, 1965).
7. See Justin Kaplan's account of Twain's courtship letters to Livy, in which he regrets giving her Don Quixote to read (*Mr. Clemens and Mark Twain, a Biography*, New York: Simon & Schuster, 1966, pp. 92–93). "It is no reading matter for girls," and "You are as pure as snow, and I would have you always so—untainted, untouched even by the impure thoughts of others," n. 93.

8. All quotes from "Tennessee's Partner" come from Bret Harte's *The Luck of Roaring Camp*. New York: Dover Thrift Editions, 1992.
9. See Bradford A. Booth's "Mark Twain's Comments on Bret Harte's Stories," *American Literature*, XXV (January 1954): 492–495.
10. See William F. Connor's "The Euchring of Tennessee: A Reexamination of Bret Harte's "Tennessee's Partner," *Studies in Short Fiction* 17 (Spring 1980): 13. Connor's argument doesn't account for the Partner's grief after his "revenge" is accomplished.
11. See Axel Nissen's *Bret Harte: Prince and Pauper*, Jackson, MS: University of Mississippi, 2000.
12. The celebrated Irish playwright and poet was convicted of "gross indecency" for engaging in sodomy in 1895.
13. Quotes from "In the Tules" are taken from *In a Hollow of the Hills and Other Tales* (vol. 10 of Stories of California and the Frontier, Boston: Houghton Mifflin, 1894, pp. 378–400).
14. Harte, Bret. "Uncle Billy and Uncle Jim," in *Stories in Light and Shadow*. Boston: Houghton Mifflin, 1898.
15. Here is the full text of "The Mammoth Cod," as published in G. Legman's book, *The Mammoth Cod*. Milwaukee, WI: Maledicta, 1976, pp. 18–22.

> I thank Thee for the bull, O God
> Whenever a steak I eat,
> The working of his mammoth cod
> Is what gives to us our meat.
>
> And for the ram, a meed of praise
> He with his mighty cod
> Foundation for our mutton lays
> With every vigorous prod.
>
> And then the boar who at his work
> His hindhoofs fixed in sod,
> Contented, packs the embryo pork
> All with his mighty cod.
>
> Of beasts, man is the only one
> Created by our God
> Who purposely, and for mere fun,
> Plays with his mammoth cod. (19)

16. According to Legman, it is impossible to tell if Twain read this letter out loud himself, or if he sent it and it was read by someone else.
17. In "Anglo-American Clubs: Their Wit, Their Heterodoxy, Their Sedition" (*The William and Mary Quarterly*, LI, 2 [April 1994] 293–304) David S. Shields discusses the uses of clubhouse ribaldry in the formation of communities in British America and the early Colonial period in North America. See also Marie Mulrey Roberts, "Pleasures Engendered by Gender: Homosociality and the Club," in *Pleasure in the Eighteenth Century*, eds. Roy Porter and Marie Malvey Roberts (New York: New York University Press, 1996).
18. See Albert Parry's book, *Garrets and Pretenders: A History of Bohemianism in America* (New York: Dover Press, 1960), especially p. 140. Widely advertised as "the national anthem of the boundless realm of Bohemia," O'Reilly's poem includes the anthem:

> I'd rather live in Bohemia than in any other land,
> For only there are the values true,
> And the laurels gathered in all men's view.

Promoting a Democratic aesthetic, the poem goes on to claim that in Bohemia, the wisest critics of art and literature are "never shrewd" and the laurels that come with fame come without "force or by deeds undone."
19. Saum's recent book does an adequate job of recovering the now-forgotten political and transitory social intrigues that were the backbone of his acid tongue.
20. Eugene Field. *Only a Boy*. 1895. Reprinted. (New York: Canyon Books, 1968).

INDEX

Adams, Andy, 59, 62
   Log of a Cowboy, The: A Narrative of the Old Trail Days, 7–8, 12, 16, 60
   Texas Matchmaker, The, 15, 59, 60
Adventures of Huckleberry Finn, The, Mark Twain, 99, 105, 110, 117
   Ellison, Ralph comment on, 4
   Feidler, Leslie on, 4
   historical accuracy of, 5
   Huck's and Jim's relationship, 4–5
   Huckleberry Finn character, 116–17
   Looby, James on, 4
African American cowboys, 16, 29
Allmendinger, Blake, 11, 17, 121*n*11, 126*n*4
American aesthetic possibilities, 73–4
American national identity, 2–3, 6, 12, 61–2
American satyriasis
   defined, 16
   Harris, Frank, 71, 80–6
   Hartland, Claude, 71, 86–93
   literary production and, 81
   and the poetics of homoeroticism, 71, 79
   Whitman, Walt, 71–80, 85
Anglo supremacy, 24
anthropological evidence, 17
Appleton's Journal, 63
Aristophanes, 33

Atlantic Monthly magazine
   on escapist literature, 61
   on Loring, Frederic, 63

Bareback Buck, Centaur of the Plains, Philip Warne, 56–7
Beardsley, Aubrey, 81
berdache term, 17, 125*n*20
Billy Budd, Sailor, Herman Melville, 57, 59
Bohemia, 110
"Boston Marriage" (male marriage), 15

Carlyle, Thomas, 81
Casey's Table d'Hôte, Eugene Field, 98, 99, 133*n*3
Chamberlain, William W., 65
characters in frontier literature (example of), 62
City of Orgies, Whitman, Walt, 74, 75
Clark, Badger C., 9, 10
Clay, Bertha (love stories of), 89, 133*n*15
Clemens, Olivia, 99–100
Clemens, Samuel Longhorne, *see* Twain, Mark
Come Back to the Raft Ag'in, Huck Honey!, Feidler, Leslie, 4
Cooper, James Fenimore, 3, 5, 15
   compared to Bret Harte, 100
   encoded homoeroticism and, 21, 23–4
   friendship and eroticism, his view of, 35–7

Cooper, James Fenimore—*continued*
  frontier experience of, 68, 129*n*23
  hybridized characters of, 28–31, 33–4
  idealized characters of, 20, 122*n*1
  influence on American culture, 19–20, 37, 40
  Irish-Americans, characterization of, 32
  Lawrence, D. H. on, 20
  Manifest Destiny doctrines and, 24, 31
  myths and, 33, 35, 36, 37
  queer partnerships and, 40
  Twain, Mark on, 20
  see also Deerslayer, The; *Leatherstocking Tales, The*; *Pilot, The*; *Pioneers, The*; *Red Rover, The*
Cowboy and Sex, The, Westermeier, Clifford P., 17
cowboy code, 42–3, 44, 46, 49–50, 98
cowboy image
  American national identity and, 12
  described, 2–3
  homoerotic affection, 3–4, 12
  masculinity and, 2, 28
  misanthrope and, 2–3, 115
  in pre-1900 literature, 1–3
  sexual abstinence in, 3
Cowitch, Shoshone chief, 63–5
cultural tolerance of same-sex relations, 56, 128*n*14
Cutler, Elbridge J., 65

Deerslayer, The, Cooper, James Fenimore, 21, 25
Doleful Ballad of the Rejected Lover, The, Mark Twain, 104
Dollimore, Jonathan, 9
Drum Taps, Walt Whitman, 74–5
Dutch Lullaby, A, Eugene Field, 110

Edelman, Lee, 9
Elder Conklin and Other Stories, Frank Harris, 85

"elemental talk of sex", 6, 43–4
  see also language about sex
Ellison, Ralph, 4
Emerson, Ralph Waldo, 3, 80, 83
eroticism
  in frontier literature, 5, 13–14, 24–8
  and men's clubs, 108–9, 116

"fag" term, 4
Feidler, Leslie, 5
  on *Adventures of Huckleberry Finn, The*, Mark Twain, 4
  on Cooper, James Fenimore, 20
femininity
  avoidance of, 55
  cowboy code and, 7–8
  cowboy identity and, 43
  "goodness" of, 49–50
  male eroticism categories and, 13
  in nature, 22–3
  in *Socratic Love*, Eugene Field, 115
  Whitman, Walt and, 75–6, 131*n*5
Field, Eugene, 16, 117
  Casey's Table d'Hôte, 98, 99, 133*n*3
  compared to Mark Twain, 110–11
  Dutch Lullaby, A, 110
  Gingham Dog and the Calico Cat, The, 110
  Little Book of Western Verse, 98, 117
  Little Boy Blue, 110, 111
  male erotic bonding and, 98
  Only a Boy, 116
  Socratic Love, 109, 111, 112–16
  Western humor and, 113–15
frontier literature
  American national identity and, 2–3, 6, 12, 61–2
  categories of male eroticism in, 13–14
  a central theme in, 6
  cowboys as hybrid figures in, 43
  cultural tolerance of same-sex relations, 56, 128*n*14
  dominant narrative in, 5
  "elemental talk of sex" in, 6, 43–4

examples of characters in, 62
femininity and, 7–8, 13, 22–3, 43, 49–50, 55
frontier, meaning of, 2–3, 119*n*3
homoerotic friendships in, 5–6
literary formula of, 2
as a literary genre, 1–2, 119*n*1
manhood in, 2, 6
masculine code in, 28
Michaels, Walter Benn on, 6
plots of, 55
Queer theory and, 9
romance motif in, 55
same-sex bonds in, 7, 28, 37
Slotkin, Richard on, 6
Smith, Ogden Nash on, 6
as teaching parables, 6
Thompkins, Jane on, 8–9
Wister, Owen revisionist of, 15, 55, 60

Gay American History, Katz, Ned, 17
Gilded Age, The, Mark Twain and Charles Dudley Warner, 99
Gillis, Steven, 104
Gingham Dog and the Calico Cat, The, Eugene Field, 110
Gray Fox Press, 86
Greek myths, 33, 35, 36, 103

Handley, William, 11
handsomeness, the effect of, 56–9
Harper's Magazine, 107
Harris, Frank, 16, 71
  affair with Smith, Byron, 82–3
  attacked for advocacy of sex, 84–5
  compared with Walt Whitman, 81
  editorship of the *Saturday Review*, 84–5
  Elder Conklin and Other Stories, 85
  Emerson, Ralph Waldo and, 83
  literary style of, 92
  Mencken, H. L. on, 85
  My Life and Loves, 80–1, 84, 85, 132*n*8
  My Reminiscences as a Cowboy, 85
  priapism of, 80–1, 82
  promiscuity and, 80–1
  ravishment of, 81–3
  on Shaw, Bernard, 81, 84
  Sinclair, Upton on, 85
  spermatorrhea and, 83, 132*n*11
  Whitman, Walt and, 83–5
  on Wilde, Oscar, 81, 85
Harte, Bret
  compared to James Fenimore Cooper, 100
  compared to Mark Twain, 100
  homoerotic relations and, 101–4
  Luck of Roaring Camp and Other Stories, The, 100
  Oscar Wilde, responds to trials of, 102, 135*n*12
  on "queer secrets", 117
  Tennessee's Partner, 100–1
  Tules, In the, 102–3
  Uncle Jim and Uncle Billy, 103–4
  Western humor and, 97, 101
Hartland, Claude, 13, 16, 71
  citizenship, imagining new forms of, 92
  compared to Frank Harris, 86
  compared to Walt Whitman, 86, 91–2
  coy pornography of, 88
  describing his ideal lover, 88–9
  "flowery language" of, 90–1
  literary influence of Clay, Bertha, 89, 133*n*15
  literary style of, 92
  male nymphomania and, 86–8, 93
  physicians and, 86–8, 93
  same-sex sexual ecstasy, 91
  Story of a Life, The, autobiography of, 13, 86, 87, 88, 89–90, 133*n*14
Harvard University, 62, 65, 66, 67, 129*n*26
Harvey, Charles M. on escapist literature, 61
heterosexuality, 6, 9

historical evidence, 16–18
  Allmendinger, Blake on, 17
  Cowboy and Sex, The, Westermeier, Clifford P., 17
  in Dodge City Police Court Docket (1885–1888), 16
  Gay American History, Katz, Ned, 17
  in Great Plains Native American tribes (*berdache*), 17, 125*n*20
  in Mormon communities, 17
  Quinn, Michael C. on, 17, 125*n*19
homoerotic
  aesthetic, 16, 73–4, 77
  affection, 3–4, 12, 13, 40
  encoded homoeroticism, 21, 23–4
  friendships, 5–6, 96–7
  harmony, 97, 101
  imagery, 78–9
  language, 6, 14, 43–4, 66, 67, 121*n*15, 125*n*19
  literary production and, 81, 92
  parable, 41–3
  partnership, 101–2, 103
  poetics and, 71, 79
"homosexual" term, 4, 56, 120*n*6
hybridism, 28–31, 33–4, 38–9

Independent publication, 63
Innocents Abroad, The, Mark Twain, 99

James, Henry, 2, 56

King, Tom, 51, 52

L.S. Matthews & Company, 86
language about sex, 14, 66, 67, 121*n*15, 125*n*19
  see also "elemental talk of sex"
Last of the Mohicans, The, Cooper, James Fenimore, 21
Lawrence, D. H., 20
Leatherstocking Tales, The, James Fenimore Cooper, 4, 13, 40
  Anglo supremacy in, 24
  bond of erotic love in, 22, 23, 25–6, 28, 123*n*6
  Bumppo/Deerslayer and Chingachgook bond, 22, 40
  Bumppo/Deerslayer character, 21, 23, 24, 25–6, 27
  Chingachgook character, 21, 22, 23, 24, 25–6, 27
  elitism in, 23–4
  encoded homoeroticism in, 21, 23–4
  erotic meanings in vocabulary, 24–6, 123*n*9
  erotic transference in, 24–8
  femininity in, 22–3
  Hutter, Judith character, 22, 23, 25
  Manifest Destiny doctrines and, 24
  March, Harry character, 25
  masculine code in, 28
  myth and, 21, 24
  nature, representation of, 22
  parental partnership in, 22, 25–6, 27–8, 31
  setting of, 21
  speech style in, 22
  Wah-ta!-Wah character, 22, 23, 25
Leaves of Grass, Walt Whitman, 57, 75
  Calamus section of, 76–7, 78, 80
  Emerson, Ralph Waldo approval of, 80
  Prairie Grass Dividing, The, 77
  Promise to California, A, 76–7
  revisions of, 80, 85
  sex-positive manifesto in, 80
  To a Western Boy quoted, 76
Legend of the Swan Maiden, The, Leavey, Barbara Fass, 39
Life on the Mississippi, Mark Twain, 99
Limerick, Patricia Nelson, 11
Little Book of Western Verse, Eugene Field, 98, 117
Little Boy Blue, Eugene Field, 110, 111
Live Boys; or Charlie and Nasho in Texas, Pilgrim, Thomas (C. J.)
  blizzard scene in, 60–1
  Captain Dick character, 37, 39
  Charley character, 37–9, 60–1

erotic quality of friendship in, 61
hybridism in, 38–9
male marriage and, 15
mythology in, 39
Nasho character, 38, 60–1
renegade horse scene, 61
reunion scene in, 39, 40
transformation in, 38–9
Log of a Cowboy, The: A Narrative of the Old Trail Days, Andy Adams, 7–8, 12, 16, 60
Looby, James, 4
Loring, Frederic, 62–5
  Chamberlain, William W. and, 65
  Cowitch, Shoshone chief and, 63–5
  death of, 63, 65, 129n27
  early career of, 62–3
  experience of the West, 62–4, 68
  imperialist privilege and, 64
Lost Pardner, The, Badger C. Clark, 9, 11
Luck of Roaring Camp and Other Stories, The, Bret Harte, 100

male camaraderie, 7–8
male eroticism categories, 13–14
male marriage ("Boston Marriage"), 15
male nymphomania, 86–7, 93
male privilege, 97, 100
Mammoth Cod, The, Mark Twain, 105–7, 116, 135n15
Mammoth Cod Club, 105–7, 116
Manifest Destiny doctrines, 3, 24, 31
manliness, 61, 62
"manly attachment" (comradeship), 71–2, 73, 74–6
marriage to women, 3, 7–8, 122n5
  rejection of, 51, 59–60
  ridicule of, 68–9
  in *Texas Matchmaker, The*, Andy Adams, 60
  in *Two College Friends*, Loring, Frederick, 66, 67, 68, 69
  in *Virginian, The*, Wister, Owen, 42–3, 44, 49–50, 68–9
masculine code in frontier literature, 28

"mastering passion", 7, 13
Maupassant, (Henri René Albert) Guy de, 81
Melville, Herman
  Billy Budd, Sailor, 57, 59
  on handsomeness, 57, 59
  Moby Dick, 4
men's clubs and eroticism, 108–9, 116
Mencken, H. L., 85
Mestizo cowboys, 17, 29, 57
Michaels, Walter Benn, 6
misanthrope, 2–3, 115
miscegenation, 6
Moby Dick, Herman Melville, 4
morality, of elite white men, 27
Murieta, Joaquín, 57
My Life and Loves, Frank Harris, 80–1, 84, 85, 132n8
My Reminiscences As a Cowboy, Frank Harris, 13, 85
myths, 20, 21, 24, 39
  Cooper, James Fenimore and, 33, 35, 36, 37
  Harte, Bret and, 103

Native American nakedness, 26–7, 123n8
Negro Cowboys, The, Durham, Philip and Everett Jones, 16
New Western History (intellectual movement), 11–12
New York Times, The, 63
Nissen, Axel on *In the Tules*, 102
Nothing but Prairie and Sky, Bruce Seiberts, 13

onanism, 107–8
Only a Boy, Eugene Field, 116
Oregon Trail, The, Francis Parkman, 26
O'Reilly, John Boyle, 109, 136n18

pantheism, 14
Papyrus Club of Boston, 109–11, 113, 114
parables, teaching of, 6
Parkman, Francis, 26

Pilot, The, James Fenimore Cooper, 19, 21
   Captain Borroughcliffe, 34, 35–6
   Captain Manual character, 34, 35–6
   deathbed kiss scene, 35–6, 124*n*16
   "fraternal love" and, 36
   utilitarian ending of, 35
   and the word "intercourse", 34
Pioneers, The, James Fenimore Cooper, 28–31, 56
   Elizabeth Temple character, 30
   Judge Temple character, 30
   Major Effingham character, 30
   Oliver Edwards character, 28–31
   queer interracial partnership in, 30
   racial purity in, 29–30
   setting of, 28
Pope, Alexander, 115
pornography, 88, 121*n*19
priapism, 78, 80, 82–3
promiscuity, 76–80
Promise to California, A, Walt Whiteman, 76–7

"queer" term, 4
Queer theory, 9, 123*n*6
Quinn, Michael C., 17, 125*n*19

racial purity, 30, 31, 32, 33
Rape of the Lock, The, Alexander Pope, 115
Red Rover, The, James Fenimore Cooper, 31–4
   Dick Fid character, 31, 32, 34
   Harry Wilder character, 31–2
   hybridism in, 33–4
   Irish-Americans, characterization of, 32
   racial otherness in, 33
   Scipio Africanus character, 31, 32–3, 34, 124*n*11
Remington, Frederic, 58
ribaldry, 96–7, 98
Roughing It, Mark Twain, 96, 99

Rousseau, Jean Jacques, 26, 42–3
Russell, Charles M., 54

same-sex bonds, 7, 28, 37
Saturday Evening Gazette, 62
Saturday Review publication, 84
Sedgwick, Eve Kosofsky, 9
Seiberts, Bruce, 13
sex-for-procreation, 6, 14
"sex hunger", 13–14
sexual elitism, 107
Shaw, Bernard, 81, 84
Shields, David on men's clubs, 108–9
Sinclair, Upton, 85
Siringo, Charles, 62, 129*n*25
"situational homosexuality", 14
Slotkin, Richard, 6
Smith, Adam, 27
Smith, Byron, 82–3
Smith, Ogden Nash, 6
Socratic Love, Eugene Field, 13
   Alcibiades character in, 114–15, 116
   burlesque in, 112–14
   construction of, 112, 116
   euphemisms in, 115
   ironic effect in, 115
   literary context of, 111
   misogynist fantasy in, 115
   and Papyrus Club of Boston, 109, 111, 113
   Socrates character in, 114, 115
   Symposium, The of Plato and, 114
   Western humor and, 113–15
   Wilson, Francis on, 109
Specimen Days, Whitman, Walt, 75
spermatorrhea, 83, 132*n*11
St. Louis Post-Dispatch, 71, 72
stag dance, 72
Story of a Life, The, Claude Hartland
   intended readership of, 86–7
   language of, 13, 89–90
   literary scholarship on, 133*n*14
   as pornography, 88
Strand, The publication, 102

Surpassing the Love of Men, Faderman, Lillian, 15
Symposium, The, Plato, 114

Tennessee's Partner, Bret Harte, 117
  homoerotic harmony and, 101
  jealousy and, 101–2
  male homoerotic partnership, promotion of, 101–2
  Mark Twain's reaction to, 101
A Texas Cowboy, Charles Siringo, 62, 129*n*25
Texas Matchmaker, The, Andy Adams
  Lance Lovelace character, 59, 60
  male marriage, 15
  rejection of marriage to women in, 60
Tompkins, Jane, 8, 11
Tules, In the, Bret Harte, 102–3
Turner, Frederick Jackson, 11
Twain, Mark, 16, 20
  Adventures of Huckleberry Finn, The, 99, 104–5, 110, 117
  Adventures of Tom Sawyer, The, 105, 117
  celebrating male privilege, 97, 100
  compared to Eugene Field, 110–11
  on deviant sexuality, 96
  Doleful Ballad of the Rejected Lover, The, 104
  friendship with Hart, Bret, 99
  Gillis, Steve and, 104
  homoerotic friendships and, 96–7, 100
  Huckleberry Finn, 116–17
  Innocents Abroad, The, 99
  Life on the Mississippi, 99
  Mammoth Cod, The, 105–7, 116, 135*n*15
  on onanism, 107–8
  on polygamy, 96
  on "queer secrets", 95–6, 104, 117
  ribaldry of, 96–7, 99–100, 105–8
  Roughing It, 96
  on sexual elitism, 107
  Stomach Club, address to, 107–8
  sub rosa material of, 97, 104, 105–8, 133*n*1
  on *Tennessee's Partner*, 101
  Western humor and, 97
Two Admirals, The, James Fenimore Cooper, 21, 31
Two College Friends, Frederic Loring, 13, 15, 62–3, 130*n*29
  Chamberlain, William W. and, 65, 66
  comparison to *Virginian, The*, Owen Wister, 68
  Cutler, Elbridge J. and, 65, 66
  homoerotic language in, 66, 67
  marriage and, 67, 68
  Ned character, 66
  preface dedication, 65
  synopsis of, 66–8
  Tom character, 66
Two Years before the Mast, Richard Henry Dana, Jr., 4

Uncle Jim and Uncle Billy, Bret Harte, 103–4
Union Catalogue of Manuscripts, The, 86

Virginian, The, Owen Wister, 2, 3, 13, 15, 18
  call of the wild riddle in, 42
  cowboy code, 42–3, 46
  "elemental talk of sex" in, 43–5
  encoded homoeroticism in, 43–6, 48–9, 53
  "goodness" of women, 49–50
  handsomeness and, 56–7
  homoerotic parable in, 41–3, 55
  James, Henry commenting on, 2, 56
  King, Tom as prototype of, 51
  as a love letter, 44
  Molly Stark Wood character, 41–2, 54–5
  narrator's relationship with, 44–6, 48–50, 53, 62

Virginian, The—continued
  rebellious ideologies and the wilderness, 55
  revision of frontier literature, 55, 60
  Steve character, 43, 44–5, 46, 62
  West, George as prototype of, 52
  Western humor and, 97
  Wister, Owen preface of, 55

Warne, Philip, 62, 128n17
West, George, 50–1, 52
Western Boy, To a, Walt Whitman, 76
Western humor, 98
  Field, Eugene, 113–15
  Harte, Bret and, 97
  Twain, Mark and, 97
West of Everything, Jane Tompkins, 8
Whitman, Walt, 13, 16, 57
  and American aesthetic possibilities, 73–4
  attacked for advocacy of sex, 85
  citizenship, imagining new forms of, 92
  City of Orgies, 74, 75
  compared to Claude Hartland, 86, 91–2
  compared to Frank Harris, 81, 84–5
  desire to teach, 76–7
  Drum Taps meditation, 74–5
  homoerotic imagery, 78–9
  "I Heard It Charged Against Me" rebuttal, 78
  Leaves of Grass, 75–80
  Leaves of Grass, Calamus section of, 76–7, 78
  literary manifesto of, 74, 130n4
  literary style of, 92
  "manly attachment" (comradeship), 71–2, 73, 74–6, 78
  originality of, 80
  Prairie Grass Dividing, The, 77
  "Prairies, The" speech and, 72–3
  predictions of, 72, 73
  promiscuity and, 76–80
  satyriasis, his promotion of, 79
  sex-positive manifesto, 78, 80
  Specimen Days, 75
  St. Louis Post-Dispatch interview, 71, 130n1
  To a Western Boy quoted, 76
  Western "eleve" of, 76, 78, 79, 80, 132n6
  women, observations of, 75, 131n5
Wilde, Oscar, 81, 84, 85, 102, 135n12
Wilson, Francis, 109
Wister, Owen, 2, 6, 15
  on cowboys and patriotic pride, 53
  erotic currents in his fiction, 47–8, 126n5
  experience of the West, 62, 68
  on handsomeness, 59
  immorality of cowboys, 53, 127n13
  journal entries of, 51
  marriage of, 50
  rejection of marriage and, 51
  revision of frontier literature, 15, 55
  transformational experience of, 50–1
  West, George and, 50–1, 52, 62
  see also Virginian, The
World publication, 63

Lightning Source UK Ltd.
Milton Keynes UK
UKOW05f1353231216
290749UK00002B/33/P